12 NOV 1992

Your Ultimate Choice

Your Ultimate Choice

The Right to Die with Dignity

EDITED BY
THE VOLUNTARY EUTHANASIA SOCIETY

Souvenir Press

First published 1992 by Souvenir Press Ltd,
43 Great Russell Street, London WC1B 3PA
and simultaneously in Canada

ISBN 0 285 63101 2

Printed in Great Britain by
Biddles Ltd, Guildford & Kings Lynn

Photoset by Rowland Phototypesetting Ltd
Bury St Edmunds, Suffolk

Contents

Acknowledgements

The editors and publishers are grateful to the following authors, agents and publishers for permission to use copyright material in this book: *The Independent* for an article by Susanne Hall (4 February 1992); Pat Challinor for a letter reprinted from *She* magazine; The Daily Telegraph plc for 'The Right to Die with Dignity' by Dirk Bogarde and 'The Slippery Slope of Euthanasia' by Gillian Tindall (© The Daily Telegraph plc, 1991/1987); Rogers, Coleridge & White Ltd for an article by Ludovic Kennedy from *The Daily Telegraph*; Dr Colin Brewer for his article from the *Sunday Times; Care of the Elderly* for 'Thoughts on Euthanasia' by Lord Soper; Peters, Fraser & Dunlop and the Estate of Arthur Koestler for Arthur Koestler's suicide letter; Jonathan Glover for 'Suicide: The Right and the Dilemma' from the *Sunday Times*; Downlander Publishing for 'In Memory of an Afghan Hound' by Eric Vio from *The Grat Divide*; *BMA News Review* for an article by Colin Brewer; British Medical Association for extracts from *Euthanasia*, the Report of the BMA Working Party, and for permission to summarise the 'BMA Statement on Advance Directives); *British Medical Journal* for extracts from 'News and Political Review: Euthanasia around the World', (*BMJ* 4 January 1992), and for the comment by the Chairman of the Voluntary Euthanasia Society on the Report of the BMA Working Party on Euthanasia (*BMJ* 1988); *Medical Monitor* for an article by Colin Brewer; *History Today* for extracts from 'The Death of King George V' by Francis Watson (December 1986); Nicholas Walter for his letter published in *The Times* (December 1986); *The Economist* for 'Die as You Choose' (5 March 1988); *Catholic Herald* for article on Italy (22 February 1985). 'Last Rights' by Pat Turton is reproduced by kind permission of *Nursing Times* where this article first appeared on 27 April 1987. 'The Quality of Dying' by Margaret Arral is reproduced by kind permission of *Nursing Times*. This article first appeared in *Nursing Mirror* on 31 July 1985. While every care has been taken to clear permission for use of the articles in this book, in the case of any accidental infringement, copyright holders are asked to contact the publishers.

Preface

Most of us dread the thought of losing our mental and physical faculties, whether through old age, serious accident or terminal illness. We would not want to be kept alive by artificial means or sophisticated drugs when all possibility of leading a useful life was gone; we would want to be allowed to die with dignity.

It is not the intention of this book to argue the case for and against euthanasia—a word that has acquired sinister connotations in the minds of some people. Its aim is to show how we may retain control of our lives until the end, ensuring that we are not subjected to life-sustaining medical treatments when we are no longer able to make our objections known.

The solution lies in the Advance Directive or Living Will, a copy of which is included at the back of this book, together with full instructions on how to use it. Produced by the Voluntary Euthanasia Society and approved by learned Counsel, it allows you to make a signed and witnessed statement, avowing your wish to be allowed to die without hindrance, treated only for pain relief, should you ever reach a state when you are beyond hope of recovery. No doctor may administer treatment against a patient's will, and the Advance Directive makes such wishes plain even if you are too ill or injured to express them verbally.

The experiences, often painful, recorded in this book make clear the need for a Living Will or Advance Directive, and the views of those prominent in the campaign for legal reform add force to a growing body of opinion that there are situations in which we would all prefer to be allowed to die in peace. This book empowers you to do so.

The Dying Patient's Bill of Rights

The right to be treated as a living human being until I die.

The right to be cared for by those who can maintain a sense of hopefulness.

The right to maintain a sense of hopefulness.

The right to express my feelings and emotions about my approaching death in my own way.

The right to participate in decisions concerning my care.

The right to expect continuing medical and nursing attention even though 'cure' goals must be changed to 'comfort' goals.

The right not to die alone.

The right to be free from pain.

The right to have my questions answered honestly.

The right not to be deceived.

The right to have help from and for my family in accepting my death.

The right to die in peace and dignity.

The right to retain my individuality and not be judged for my decisions which may be contrary to the beliefs of others.

The right to discuss and enlarge my religious and spiritual experiences, whatever these may mean to others.

The right to expect that my body will be treated after death as I want it to be.

The right to be cared for by caring, sensitive, knowledgeable people who will attempt to understand my needs and will be able to gain some satisfaction in helping me face my death.

The right to decide when I am ready for death and to have that decision acted upon.

1
Let Me Go

To save a man against his will is the same as killing him.

Ars Poetica. HORACE

It is two years since my 78-year-old widowed mother fell from the racehorse that she was riding side-saddle. She never recovered. And it is a month since my mother-in-law, 91 years old, had a massive stroke from which *she* will never recover. The anguish and suffering imposed on them both leaves me in no doubt that euthanasia is a subject which must be addressed if doctors are to offer treatments that are both advanced and humane.

Taken from the roadside to Hereford Hospital, my mother was then transferred to the neurology centre at Smethwick, in the West Midlands. My son and I had little inkling of the horrors that lay ahead as we followed the ambulance through the fog. A request at 3am for my consent to brain surgery for my mother had me asking all those questions that prompt ambiguous replies from doctors.

Her life's motto had always been 'leave it to nature'. I'd been exhorted never to let her be 'wired up to any of that machinery' so my inclination was to say 'No.' Would she, if I said 'Yes,' be mentally impaired, unable to speak, reduced to an existence instead of a life? The answers left me with no choice. Pressure on her swelling brain must be eased immediately, restoring consciousness within 48 hours, or she would suffer irreversible damage.

After the surgery, my mother sank deeper into a coma. Instruments monitored her condition, the doctors anticipated her demise and I called on the Deity to hasten it. Five and a half weeks later she came round. The surgical prelude was

9

over, and eight months of attempts at rehabilitation were to follow. Unable to move or talk, she slowly assembled her badly-impaired faculties so that she could at least recognise me and her grandchildren.

Superbly nursed, with daily physiotherapy, she was soon off the danger list and therefore ineligible for her bed in the specialist unit. Still zombie-like, she was transferred from the unit to a general ward.

I could not continue commuting to Birmingham twice a week indefinitely. And when I found her one day slumped in a chair with her face in her lunch, I insisted not only that she be put back to bed forthwith, but also that she must be moved to Norfolk where I could visit her daily.

The ambulance strike was at its height, so I hired a private ambulance to transport her to the local cottage hospital near home. There she was as diligently nursed as anyone could wish. She struggled with mobility exercises, learned to write illegibly and to speak coherently. She and I attempted to assemble jigsaw puzzles designed for five-year-olds, and to play snap.

She hadn't laughed since her accident and never did so again. Soon I was able to bring her home each day, heaving her from car to wheelchair to chaise-longue. An avid gardener all her life, she amazed me by correctly naming plants such as hellebores, while remaining unable to master the television switch. Walking was beyond her; her lack of balance precipitated nausea and vomiting, and caused great distress. Next came the decision as to her long-term future, and I visited various recommended homes.

My mother was transferred to her own room in a purpose-built, well-staffed nursing home. When I asked her if she was pleased to be there she replied, 'I'd rather be in a coffin.' She continued to come home for the day, despite increasing car-sickness during the six-mile journeys. Fatigue and nausea plagued her as did chest and urinary infections.

Her fellow patients included a pitiful 90-year-old ex-missionary. Once the venerated principal of an Indian station and author of several books, she was now a crumpled rag-doll on a bean-bag. Unable to communicate or even feed herself, and unsafe in a chair, she spent her days in isolation.

Gradually, my mother's physical condition and her diminished mental capacity deteriorated even further. Hours spent in sleep became days spent in sleep. This once energetic and fit woman who had lived alone in the country surrounded by her animals, who had ridden every day, painted flowers prodigiously, and drove hundreds of miles to go racing, was now chairbound. Her once-capable hands lay twitching in her lap.

Soon she was to be bedbound, the recipient of repeated antibiotics to keep pneumonia at bay. When bed-sores necessitated her transference to a mesh hammock slung above her bed and on which she could be rolled hourly, all she could do was hold my hand and make occasional eye contact which spelt 'Please . . . '

Distraught and tearful I visited the nursing-home doctor to insist that he stop treating her for recovery, concentrating instead on her comfort. I didn't ask him to kill my mother, merely not to hinder her dying. She did so six days later. It could, and should, have been sooner.

My mother-in-law is a dear, proud and independent old lady. She has frequently told me in serious as well as jocular mood, that she is looking forward to dying and rejoining, amongst others, Tom, her beloved son and my late husband. She has remained adamant that no one must ever put her 'in one of those old people's places', and devoted neighbours have made this avoidable. Armed with an emergency button she has survived several falls and two broken hips. Almost blind and only able to shuffle about on a zimmer, or be pushed in a wheelchair, she enjoyed and gave great pleasure to her doting family.

Four weeks ago she was found unconscious after a stroke, and deep in coma, she hovered between life and death, for five days. But no one could possibly help Granny to die; instead, they are helping her to 'recover'. In hospital I found her the saddest relic of humanity that I have ever seen. This blind and paralysed old lady, unable to speak, only to grunt, was crumpled in an uncomfortable chair. I pressed her bell (she could not) and asked (she could not) that she be put back to bed. Her relief was pitiful and she slept at once. Blissful oblivion from now on? Oh no! Next came talk of physiotherapy to help mobility.

Once again distraught, I confronted one of the young doctors on the ward who repeated all that I'd heard before. But at least he assured me that antibiotics would not be prescribed.

So why can't she be spared all the hauling and mauling out of bed into the wretched chair? Yes, you've got it. It's better for the lungs. Cruellest of all is that she has retained her excellent hearing, and understands all that is said. Overjoyed to hear a familiar voice, she clutches family visitors with her left hand, the only limb she is able to move, poignantly transmitting confusion and fear. Coward that I am, I tell her that it won't be long now. And indeed it won't.

Soon she is in transit again. The doctors think that she has reached her 'ceiling' of recovery, and could live bedbound, paralysed, mute and blind for weeks, months or even years. But where? Saved from the grave by medical expertise she is no longer eligible for her hospital bed. Her family must make alternative long-term plans.

Calling on the Almighty again seems pretty hopeless. I do call instead on the medical profession. Pledged to preserve life, they seem unable to distinguish that from delaying death. While the former is commendable, the latter is obstructive and cruel. New guidelines must be drawn up. One enlightened doctor has assured me that compassionate and wise doctors can only help a terminally ill patient to die if they are at home, away from surveillance in hospital. Nor do patients have the option of helping themselves by declining medication, if they have surrendered responsibility for their care to others. Thus it is that the vulnerable who need the most, get the least assistance on their final journey. Forceps, epidurals, and caesarians ease our passage into the world. What is there to ease our paths from it?

SUSANNE HALL

*   *   *

The life of Isobel Lejeune could have been almost perfect, in human terms. Until she was 89, she had never had any illness, except the minor discomfort of a cold. She and her husband lived their gentle, obscure lives, undemanding, happy. No violent emotional disturbances—even their siblings lived long into old age. She was just another loving wife and mother—and filled her life with all the little repetitive tasks like millions of others—important only to the handful of people who knew and loved her. Her husband, who also had good health, died within a few hours, no lingering illness, about six months before her 89th birthday.

She was sitting quietly watching the birds in the garden, when she suddenly collapsed into a coma—and we were sad, but happy that the inevitable end had come so kindly.

Then the nightmare began. The doctor came, found she was still breathing, although quite unconscious, and she was rushed to hospital, where we had to leave her. We went back next day, thinking to find her quietly slipping away.

But modern technology can be such a dangerous thing. The doctors found they could force that tired little body to exist— so, obedient to their shortsighted, unthinking, conditioned behaviour, they did so.

She was more or less conscious, but never again coherent, or able to recognise us without confusion. She was incontinent; she had to be fed. They could not keep her in control until they put her in a bed with bars. Meanwhile, she fell often. Three times she broke an arm, on another occasion her hip—and several times we received a telephone call asking us to visit immediately, as she had fallen and was suffering severe bruising.

To visit her was anguish—to see her sitting, perhaps with an arm in a sling, and the quiet tears running down her pathetic little face, so bewildered and unhappy. This situation went on for nearly three years until just before Christmas even technology had to yield to Nature.

We despise a system that can inflict such pointless mental and physical pain. This experience has changed our whole outlook: we dread to find ourselves in the power of such people.

PEGGY LEJEUNE

*   *   *

My brother has just died. He was almost 51. I have no other brothers or sisters, and I loved him very dearly, yet when the phone call came, I said, 'Thank God.'

A year ago, he discovered he had lung cancer. Surgery was out of the question. He was told that success against cancer could very much depend on the quality of the fight put up. So he fought. Between chemotherapy sessions, he strove to force his poor, collapsed lungs to function. From small beginnings, when he had to stop to regain breath at the end of the road, he and the dog ultimately walked 12 miles a day. The flat didn't stretch him enough, so he drove to the hills and walked there. Once his hair had finished dropping out— result of the treatment—he swam at the local baths, a mile twice a week.

Weeks passed, then months, and we all dared to hope. Chest X-rays were suddenly, gloriously clear. He and his wife booked a holiday. During it, he suffered unaccountable headaches, but returned looking well and happy. Three weeks after he went back to work, it was found that the cancer had spread to his brain. Days later, he was unable to digest food. It had spread to his liver.

During six weeks of heartbreaking deterioration, which he had foreseen and dreaded, this large, cheerful, valiant man became skeletal and thrashed and twitched uncontrollably as the disease ate into his brain. Under massive doses of morphine and sedatives he was, so we were assured, unaware and suffering no pain. He was a proud, private man and would have hated us to sit and watch him as he was— but what could we do? We couldn't leave him to lie there and die alone. Everyone who was dear to him—his wife, teenaged children, his mother and all his faithful friends— longed for him to die. In distress, I begged the young doctor who had given him yet more drugs, to give him something to end it all. She said (as she had to) that this is not legal in this country.

In many ways, we were lucky. Our final ordeal lasted only about ten days. My heart goes out to those who have months to endure. Obviously we are grateful that medical practice has learnt to control pain. But wouldn't humanity be better served by permitting a compassionate end to be put to a life where only suffering or a drug-induced coma are the purposeless alternatives?

PAT CHALLINOR

THE RIGHT TO REFUSE TREATMENT

In 1988 a case came up at Ontario High Court, brought by a Jehovah's Witness against a doctor who had given her a blood transfusion while she was unconscious. In accordance with the tenets of her faith, she had been carrying a card stating quite clearly that she should not be given a transfusion under any circumstances, but her wishes had been ignored.

The court ruled that the doctor had acted wrongly, and the judge's statement made an important point:

> A conscious, rational patient is entitled to refuse any medical treatment and the doctor must comply, no matter how ill-advised he may believe that instruction to be. The doctor lawfully invades the patient's body for the purpose of treatment only after he has fully communicated to the patient the risks of treatment and the patient makes the affirmative decision, premised on a reasonable appreciation and awareness of the risks, to permit that treatment for his body. Otherwise such treatment is a battery with liability consequences.

The defence had been that the doctrine of informed consent should be extended to informed refusal, particularly since obeying the patient's wishes would have put her life at risk and, since she was unconscious, it was impossible to advise her of this. The doctor had felt he was not bound by her refusal of treatment, but the judge ruled otherwise:

> The doctrine of informed consent does not extend to informed refusal. The written direction contained in the card was not properly disregarded on the basis that circumstances prohibited verification of that decision as

an informed choice. The card constituted a valid restriction of Dr Shulman's right to treat the patient and the administration of blood by Dr Shulman did constitute battery.

More recently, in the United States, a patient sued a hospital for saving his life against his known wishes. Edward H. Winter would probably have died of a heart attack at the age of 82, if a nurse at a Cincinnati hospital had not revived him through electric shock. It was not the fate he had wanted.

A few months earlier he had watched the slow, agonising death of his wife of 55 years, who had suffered brain damage after shock resuscitation from a heart attack of her own, and he had resolved that nothing like that would happen to him. When his time came, he told his children, they should simply let him die, and he told his doctor the same thing.

The resuscitation plunged him into a nightmare more terrible than he could have imagined. Two days after he was revived, he suffered a debilitating stroke. He was left partly paralysed and largely confined to his bed in a nursing home, and although he could still speak, he was so full of despair that he could only utter a few words before he began to cry. Two years later, still enduring an existence he had dreaded, he filed a lawsuit against the hospital.

Although there have been many right-to-die lawsuits in the United States, the case brought by Mr Winter was the first 'wrongful life' case filed by a patient. It charged the hospital for failing to follow his instructions and with battery for giving him a jolt of electricity without his authorisation. But for the hospital's intervention, he declared, he could have died and with dignity.

'There are in fact some things worse than death, and what has happened to Mr Winter is one of them,' said his lawyer. 'Mr Winter had a total and unchallengeable right to decide what kind of medical care he wanted. The hospital should have been more careful to see that his decision was honoured.'

THE RIGHT TO DIE WITH DIGNITY

Desperate people write to me, slip notes under my door or stop me in the street. Never is it to say 'thank you for your book' or 'you were funny in so and so,' but to ask 'could you help?' They have a dying parent in shrieking pain, or daughter or relative who has been in a horrific traffic accident and they are in despair.

It is extraordinary. Friends I have known for years now talk about how much they want to die peacefully and with dignity. They believe, as I do, that so long as we are *compos mentis*, we must be allowed the right to decide—but only as a last resort—to be assisted to die peacefully. Before I spoke out they did not like to bring up the subject because in this country, I believe, euthanasia is still as much a taboo as talking about anti-semitism.

People may, as I have, sign an advance declaration or 'living will' to the effect that they do not want life-prolonging treatment if there is no chance of recovery from severe illness or they are incapable of rational existence. They also have a right to expect sufficient doses of pain-killers to relieve intolerable distress.

Even so, a doctor may only ease the path to the end. He cannot lawfully assist or deliberately speed up death with lethal doses of pain-killers. That is the grey area where death may be either eased or appallingly prolonged. And it is where there is a great deal of hypocrisy, particularly by doctors, many of whom are critical of me.

That is precisely what we must discuss more openly. One poll shows that nearly half of GPs would be prepared to assist death in appropriate circumstances if it were legal.

Of course there are 'good' doctors; kind and thoughtful people. One such helped the aunt of a friend. This gentle religious woman was dying hideously with cancer and in such pain she pleaded with us over and over to be let go. We sat in her kitchen with the gramophone on trying to cover the noise of her deep anguish. Eventually the Roman Catholic nurse was instructed to give her a larger dose of pain-killer, followed by another larger dose.

It is not self-aggrandisement that has led me to take a public stance. If I was not also able to say, 'I have seen screaming pain,' if I had not nursed it, seen the utter ruination it can cause both to the patient and those who care for them, or if I had not been asked to terminate a life, I would not be so vehement about the need to help people who are begging for death.

I experienced the despair when my partner and manager of 50 years lay dying in London, totally paralysed with Parkinson's disease and terminal cancer and virtually speechless. He was not shrieking, but was in deep, dire distress. When we lived in France I had promised that I would help him, but he had not put his request in writing, and we did not know about signing a 'living will'.

I would have done something—though I could not have stood in a court and proved that was what he wanted—but eventually he slipped into a coma. Almost his last words as his night nurse and myself turned him were: 'If you did this to a dog they'd arrest you.'

My views were formulated as a 24-year-old officer in Normandy. The jeep in front of us went up and we flung ourselves down a bank. There was this chap in the long grass beside me and all I could make out were the words, 'Help me, kill me'. He had no arms, face, or legs. I took out my revolver, but as I did so he was taken away and somebody else dealt with him—I heard the noise.

As the war went on, I saw more people taking the law into their own hands and I was convinced by this and later natural selections that there is no sanctity of life in existing in great pain if you are never going to get better, or will be on a life-support machine for ever, if your choice is to go. People in that state who say 'let me go' are not afraid. One friend was so paralysed by a stroke the only evidence of any movement was a tear. Perhaps without modern medicine she could not have been kept alive.

We are told that no one need put up with or die in intolerable pain. That is absolute bunk. People do die in pain and you can't imagine the hideousness of it. Hospices are admirable in helping terminally ill people to a peaceful death, but they are not available for all, and pain relief at home can be appallingly ineffective.

I know that some people find the idea of active voluntary euthanasia morally reprehensible. Nor do I deny that there are different approaches to dying. For instance, Lee Remick, my friend of nearly 35 years, who died bitterly of cancer recently, would never have asked anyone to hasten her end. She was that kind of woman and fought to hang on.

But there are changing views about the current way of death and it is time to talk about them. If we continue bringing people before the courts and exonerate—or convict—when they have carried out a 'mercy killing', we will simply bundle on as before and brush the whole issue under the carpet.

Many politicians are terrified in case showing support for voluntary euthanasia makes them unpopular with their voters. Yet polls show that most people are in favour. Of course abuse is possible. Thus any change in the law must be accompanied by proper protection, as in Holland. It is also important to state that nowhere does the Voluntary Euthanasia Society advocate getting rid of handicapped babies or the elderly or infirm.

When it comes to it, I believe we are all quite capable of being trusted with making decisions about our own lives. We did not choose to be born, but it is our privilege, I believe, to decide how we enjoy, endure and finally end our lives.

DIRK BOGARDE

PAIN OR PEACE
A case against unnecessary suffering

Like it or not, we have given non-church members the clear impression that God disapproves strongly of easing the sufferings of anybody dying from a terminal illness such as cancer.

Like other parish ministers far removed from rarified academic or moral talkshops, I work among and communicate with ordinary folk both inside and outside my congregation and it came as a surprise to discover that euthanasia aroused passionate discussion in all sections of the community. Not for the first time it was borne in upon me that the Kirk has no monopoly on compassion and indeed, judging by the reaction of many 'outsiders' we are markedly lacking in this commodity in respect of terminal suffering.

There is a fear of death around in too many quarters of the church; a fear which is based on medieval superstition and quite untouched by the glorious light of the Resurrection story.

A hangover from earlier times when the Church taught that God caused people to die still clouds the emotions of many folk in pulpit and in pew. 'Forasmuch as it hath pleased Almighty God to take unto Himself the soul of . . . ' attributes death from cancer or drunk driving or senile decay to the Father we tell the world is the essence of Love. And the world shakes its head wonderingly, or shrugs its shoulders and wants nothing to do with such a God.

I am not surprised. We of all people ought not to be afraid of death—or of discussing it. And this refusal to discuss is firmly rooted in the mistaken belief that God wills some of us to suffer long and lingeringly and thereby to cause needless grief to our loved ones. I suspect that our fear of death is reflected in our unwillingness to discuss the merits and demerits of euthanasia.

Now I well realise that there are patients and doctors who are opposed to euthanasia on principle and I respect their stand. By the same token therefore, those of us who are involved, whether as doctor or minister, in helping terminally ill people to die peacefully and with dignity have a right to receive similar respect for our wishes. I believe that no person or group of persons, however well-intentioned, should have the right to dictate terms of dying to the incurably ill. If anyone believes on conscience sake that he should die without the merciful help of drugs, then he must be free to do so. But it is quite wrong to demand that others who do not share his belief follow the same course.

It has been argued that good hospice care would be the answer.

This is not so in every case even were the facilities available and nowhere is there a hospice with the space to care for that equally humiliating and humiliated example of humanity—the so-called human vegetable kept alive purely by life-support systems.

Again it has been argued that it is the Christian duty to face maximum pain, even if that pain can be eradicated by medical skills. I would dearly like to take some of euthanasia's opponents to some bedsides in hospitals where both relatives and staff are nearly driven frantic by the pleas for release from severely ill patients—a release they look upon as the supreme gift because of what they are having to undergo. To argue that it is 'the Christian duty' to conquer pain is fine when the loved one is going into a gentle, peaceful decline. But the suggestion becomes a mockery of empty words when you are confronted with a man or woman literally screaming for death.

This is not purely an emotional reaction on my part—it is a hard and at times bitter experience of the harsh facts surrounding terminal illness in many cases. Doctors and nurses are helpless and the minister is merely the impotent symbol of a belief that suffering here will be rewarded with glory there. 'Dying well' sounds splendidly admirable in the committee-room but it has no place in the face of the realities of the hospital ward.

EAN SIMPSON
Minister of Kerse Church, Grangemouth

DIARY

Ascension weekend at home.
I take everything in, between spasms of inability to eat
And spells of being unable to see;
The trees, golden rain, the roses in bud;
Bobo the cat, who is getting old and can no longer lie on me;
My husband and daughter, who care for me so lovingly;
The District Nurse, who washes me;
All the things I can no longer reach or have brought to me;
My Doctor, to whom I try to talk softly.
She hasn't the faintest idea how my condition has worsened,
Not even that I can no longer walk;

I try to keep my cool, but fail.
Quietness, which I still enjoy, with the cooing of the doves;
The grief we share, the honesty, the tears of impotence.
It all comes too late, alas.
We've had such a good, such an exciting life.
Now the doctor can only say 'Life is suffering.'
But I've had enough suffering, can't take any more, don't
    need any more.
We're all up the creek.
My one wish is to survive in the thoughts of all who are dear to
    me
As the person I was before pain began;
It's the quality, not the quantity, that counts.
Grant me to go gently, in a worthy manner, so that all that
I've been able to give may be able to grow;
That is what I want.

From *Euthanatos*
Translation by Peter Mackay

2

In My Own Time

I will not relinquish old age if it leaves my better parts intact. But if it
begins to shake my mind, if it destroys my faculties one by one, if it
leaves me not life but breath, I will depart from the putrid and
tottering edifice. If I know that I must suffer without hope of relief I
will depart not through fear of pain itself but because it prevents all
for which I would live.

De Ira. Seneca the Younger

I suppose most of us have become attracted to the idea of
voluntary euthanasia as the result of some personal experience, either through having some close relative or friend who,
having neared the end of their days, longs to die and yet
cannot, or in the case of the medical profession, having
observed not just one person in this condition but hundreds.

In my case it was my mother.

I visited her in the nursing home where she spent the last
few years of her life. She said, 'I'm riddled with arthritis, I'm
practically bedridden and I can barely see.' Then she said,
'I've had a wonderful life and enjoyed every minute of it—
but' (and here she smiled and used a euphemism about death
which genteel Scots use and which has always been a joke in
our family) 'it's high time,' she said, 'I was gathered.'

The wish to be gathered was one she often expressed from
that time on, either to myself or my sisters, but it was to be
another ten months before it was fulfilled. It happened suddenly in the middle of the night, at a time when I was some 400
miles away and was given the news by a sympathetic but
impersonal member of the nursing home staff.

And I thought then, and I've thought many times since,
that my mother should have been allowed to go when she
wanted to go, that all the safeguards having been taken care

of by legal and medical advisers—and safeguards are very important—she could have summoned her nearest and dearest round her bedside, opened a bottle of champagne, and in an atmosphere of total love taken a suitable pill from the doctor and bidden us all farewell.

We would have grieved deeply of course, but what is wrong with that? Grief at a time of parting is necessary, and better surely for the family to weep together than separately 400 miles away as a result of a telephone call in the middle of the night.

In most countries of the Western world there is now a growing realisation that modern medicine, in increasing our span of living, has increased our span of dying too: and we all know, or know of, those who feel that because of cardiac resuscitators, antibiotics, and so on, they are now being obliged to linger on beyond their natural term.

It is not always pain (which can be largely controlled) that causes old people with terminal illnesses to lose the will to live, but the indignities and discomfort of incontinence, bed-sores, nausea and vomiting, sleeplessness, breathlessness, utter fatigue and all the other ills that ancient flesh is heir to— *in toto* an increasing deterioration of mind and body amounting to total loss of personality, as distressing for them to suffer as for their loved ones to witness.

It is tragic that so many people have to die as they do. It is tragic that there are so many genuine mercy killings, even if their perpetrators are acquitted at trial. It is tragic that those brave doctors (and I have met some) who give a patient the quick end they seek cannot do so without commiting a crime and putting their career in jeopardy.

But attitudes are changing. A Mass-Observation poll in Britain in 1969 showed that 51 per cent of the population were in favour of voluntary euthanasia, but by 1988 this had risen to 78 per cent, and in other western countries the trend is the same.

Among British doctors 35 per cent (mostly young ones) have said they would practise it when asked, if legal, and a further 10 per cent said they might do so. And a distinguished standing committee on medical ethics was quoted by *The Lancet* recently as declaring that there was nothing unethical in a doctor helping to end the life of a terminally ill patient who had asked for it.

Unfortunately many people, perhaps most, today still believe that euthanasia means others (relatives or doctors) deciding when a patient is to die. But those of us who are advocates of voluntary euthanasia cannot advocate too strongly that the only person who can demand it is the terminally ill patient him- or herself.

In Holland, where voluntary euthanasia has been practised for many years, the patient must be told his condition is incurable; his request for euthanasia must be in writing and witnessed; it must be sustained, yet can be cancelled at any time; the next of kin must be informed but can neither veto nor authorise it; the patient's doctor must consult with another unknown to him.

All of us when healthy should sign a Living Will or Advance Directive declaring that if we ever suffer loss of mental or bodily control and are judged to be beyond recovery, we do not wish to be kept artificially alive by drugs or machines. This is not yet legally enforceable but does give a doctor a guide as to one's wishes.

The objections to voluntary euthanasia are what they have always been: a belief that life is sacrosanct (in few societies has it ever been); that only God who gave life can take it away (our society is now mostly secular); that it is interfering with nature (so is removing an appendix or tumour); that hospices are a preferable alternative (there are 150,000 cancer deaths a year but fewer than 2,000 beds in hospices).

All have a common origin: fear. But the age-old irrational fear of voluntary euthanasia sliding into compulsory euthanasia has now been superseded by a greater fear: the possibility of facing a slow death of degraded senility, wired to a machine, all love of living gone.

It is wrong for those of us who love life to deny to those who have lost all relish for it the oblivion they seek. For them— and we must respect it, however hard it may be—death is a consummation devoutly to be wished; and we would be selfish and less than human not to grant it to them.

LUDOVIC KENNEDY

* * *

Most old people value above all their independence and the secure familiarity of their own home. Well-meaning but wrong-headed attempts to move them into a residential home where they can be 'properly looked after' may result in total disorientation, mental and physical breakdown and the loss of will to live.

This was the tragedy that struck an old lady of 94. Almost blind, she was nevertheless mentally alert and enjoyed tending her garden and a brisk walk to church each Sunday. As time went on she did begin to find it more difficult to manage, but she was still content to stay in her own home.

The Social Services, however, thought otherwise. They tried to persuade her to go into a 'beautiful residence for the blind', and although she refused they persisted. Distressed and desperate, she resisted with all her strength. Three times she tried to commit suicide: once by starving herself, once by putting her head in the gas oven and finally by trying to drown herself in her bath. Each time she was rescued.

Then authority took over. She was taken against her will to the institution she dreaded, and there her mind really did break; confused and unhappy she ended her life in the greatest misery, in the ward of a local hospital.

Because Society insisted on 'rescuing her from herself', she knew the ultimate horror of old age: being buried alive in an institution while her mind was still active.

With acknowledgements to G. L. HAYNES

*   *   *

That I should come to this strange place,
To finish up my days,
O God, I prayed for help that I
Might fit in with their ways.

I've washed, I've dressed, I've stood, I've sat,
I've learned to toe the line;
My mouth is checked, eyes swabbed, nails cut,
To suit the nurses' time.

I've smiled at 'Pop' and 'Dad' and 'Dear'
They mean it well I know,
But will I ever hear my name
Before I have to go?

The staff are few and they are rushed,
And mostly they are kind,
They walk me, bath me, feed my frame,
But do not feed my mind.

Deaf ears, dim eyes, imprison me,
Just memories remain;
But they are not enough, O Lord,
Please take me whence I came.

I have been—I am—grateful still
For food and warmth and light,
But now I have no dignity,
No privacy, no right.

We even have our bottoms wiped,
In full view of the ward,
I used to say 'Please screen me off';
My words were never heard.

The patients say a nurse was blamed,
For letting someone fall.
So now the screens are stored away,
And they can watch us all.

Today I soiled my pants and chair,
Is this the end for me?
The lost control—was this a sign
Of my senility?

No, it was not my fault at all,
I called the nurse for sure,
But she was busy, said to wait,
She'd see me to the door.

Was I so helpless, burdensome?
The family sent me here.
I only asked to share their home,
To feel my loved ones near.

That first sad time when Dot had gone,
They seemed to want me there,
I smoked outside, I held my tongue,
And never took his chair.

But soon their feelings changed for me,
Their eyes said 'In the way—
We can't go out, the car's too small,
No friends can come and stay.'

My daughter brings me cakes for tea.
Old Ben he shares them too.
He's grateful for these little crumbs—
For me they will not do.

I long to be myself again,
To make tea when I will
To take a walk outside and touch
A growing daffodil.

Dear Lord, I beg you take me home,
They've taken all my pride.
That leaves me with humility—
Enough to come inside?

Patient in a geriatric hospital

*　　*　　*

I am a single woman of 85 years. For some months I have had a strong feeling that my time in this world is now at an end . . . A notice came to me, only yesterday, through my local doctor, telling me an operation could be performed successfully and permanently in about three or four weeks. But what does 'permanently' mean at 85? I feel that even if the operation were entirely successful, what life would there be for me to come back to? . . . I fear the inevitable pain of such an operation might derange my mind. I dread this more than anything. Behind all this is emptiness, depression and unhappiness (the feeling of having overstayed your welcome at a party).

ANON.

*　　*　　*

There must be many of us, past the three-score-years and ten mark and with various disabilities, who feel, as Mary Stott expresses it, that the time has come 'to lay down our heavy load'. We have had an active life and now face a future of the downhill path into immobility and passive dependence on others.

As far as I know, I am not suffering from what is known as a terminal illness; only the logical consequences of an inherited dislocation of the hips, which was mistakenly treated in infancy. This condition was newly known at the time and orthopaedic surgeons were over-enthusiastic. I am in a powered wheelchair outdoors but still on my feet—just—leaning on a tea-trolley and grab-rails indoors. One fall and the next step is a nursing home.

Children and grandchildren, now independent and busy, are sympathetic and attentive but simply had no idea of why I feel this would be a fate worse than death.

EVELYN FORD

*   *   *

I believe as profoundly in the right to death as I believe in the right to life. So I believe that when it is not possible for a person who shares this conviction to take action upon it when his life is intolerable, Society should not deny him aid, any more than any civilised community would deny help to the oldest and the youngest, the poorest and the most frail, to survive.

There may be one or two of us who become so incapacitated by a stroke that we shall not be able to unscrew the top of our bottle of pills, or who are so afflicted by arthritis that we cannot raise a cup to our lips. There may be one or two of us who having contracted cancer or some other incurable illness are nursed night and day. And there may even be one or two of us who suffer the worst fate of all, the sort of brain damage we call senility or even senile dementia, so that we cease to be fully human and cannot even formulate the will to die.

For all people like this we need enabling legislation. In 1969 the Voluntary Euthanasia Society helped to formulate and promote a Bill in the House of Lords which was lost by only 61 votes to 49. In that year a Mass Observation Poll revealed that 51 per cent of those questioned were in favour of voluntary euthanasia for people who were incurable and in pain. In 1976 a similar poll found that 69 per cent of those questioned agreed that 'the law should allow adults to receive medical help to an immediate peaceful death if suffering from incurable illness that is intolerable to them, provided they have previously requested such help in writing.'

I believe that opinion is moving now even more strongly towards legalising the right to die—even among doctors and clergy. As long ago as the 1940s Dean Inge of St Paul's said: 'I do not think we can assume that God wills the prolongation of torture for the benefit of the soul of the sufferer'. In 1980 Dr Murphy, the Roman Catholic Archbiship of Cardiff, said in a radio discussion in which I took part, 'I don't tolerate, I cannot stand, extraordinary means of keeping cabbages alive by some sort of mechanical means.'

I do not want to suffer agonising pain, I do not wish to linger helplessly, incapable of movement, most of all I do not wish to lose my wits. But even more than that I do not want to see my beloved family suffer on my account. I have been told by one of my oldest and dearest friends that she would think it her duty to live on even in pain and suffering so that her sons would not be deprived of the grace of caring for her in her last years. That may be Christian doctrine, though I doubt it, but I am certainly not prepared to put my own family to the test in that way. Perhaps I could summon up the courage to endure agonising pain. What I could not endure would be to watch *my family* tortured by my pain, or helplessly pitying me. Most of all I believe that I do not have a duty to live on into the sort of decrepitude which would make me an intolerable burden. I cannot possibly believe that it would be good for my soul or theirs to see them first wincing and suffering and finally perhaps even resenting the burden of keeping me alive against my expressed will.

I believe I have an absolute moral right to say to my doctor while I am still in sound health and in full possession of my faculties: If I cannot take action to end my own life when I am no longer fully a human being, I entrust to you the duty of carrying out my wish to end it with the least possible suffering to me and my family. I want my family to be able to think of me always with love and gratitude. I hope that if I leave them by my own decision I shall be able to relieve them of any shadow of guilt. I would have them—and all of us—remember, 'Greater love hath no man than this, that a man lay down his life for his friends.'

But why should we persist in this extraordinary idea that it is better in all circumstances to be alive than dead? Why should we be afraid to die at the proper time? When I took part in a euthanasia debate at the Cambridge Union and made this point about not being afraid of death the 'leader of the opposition', the Archbishop of Liverpool, sitting opposite to me said quietly, 'No, I look forward to it.' The Victorians looked forward to 'going to a better place'. Millions of Christians, Jews, Muslims and others have envisaged a future life that would be better than this one. Lord Soper, a former president of the Methodist Church, recently recalled that his own father, at the end of his 'full and saintly life', complained bitterly that 'doctors were hindering his approach to the celestial world'.

Not all of us believe in a celestial world. Not all of us believe in any kind of personal survival. But whether we think of death as an end or a beginning there is certainly not nearly as much reason to fear it as is assumed. A friend recently said to me, 'I think we talk too much about death.' I replied, 'I think we don't talk about it nearly enough.' I think that the churches and all humanist groups ought to help us to accept the idea that death may be a doorway into something *other*— possibly something better. There are universes upon universes; there is the unimaginable vastness of the Cosmos. There is the music of the spheres. Even if after death there is no recognition—in some way we cannot now imagine—of the presence of those we have loved so much here on earth, there is surely the possibility that the caterpillar may find itself transmuted into a butterfly?

May I end with a quotation from John Masefield: 'Death opens unknown doors. It is most good to die.'

MARY STOTT

ELDERLY PATIENTS

Guidelines for the relatives of patients nearing 80 or more
who are faced with a major operation

*Read this carefully, pause awhile, make no hasty decision
and bear the following points in mind*

1 All major operations are by their nature an 'aggressive' form of treatment, some more so than others, particularly where the elderly are concerned.

2 No operation is undertaken without the expectancy of the patient's survival and the policy of treatment is, therefore, one of 'maximum recovery', even if it involves resuscitation, the use of artificial breathing apparatus, and so on.

3 No operation is performed solely for the relief of pain, as there are other ways of giving some relief to this.

4 With the advance of medical science surgeons and anaesthetists now have the backing of sophisticated aids to their skills in the operating theatre in the way, for example, of heart-monitoring apparatus; this undoubtedly improves the chances of the patient's survival.

5 After the operation the policy of 'maximum recovery' may require the patient to be placed on an artificial breathing machine, which involves passing a tube down the throat to the lungs to replace, for the time being, natural breathing.

6 It may also be necessary for the patient to be taken to the intensive care unit where, together with excellent nursing, all the latest medical technology is available to sustain and promote life, for example:

   (a) the patient may be breathing through an oxygen and humid air mask;

   (b) the patient will probably need one or more multiple drip feeds introduced through a vein, such as:

   (i) plasma;
   (ii) saline;
   (iii) antibiotics;

   (c) Drainage tubes, according to the nature of the operation, may also be necessary, such as:

   (i) from the site of the operation;
   (ii) a naso-gastric tube;

      (iii) a catheter to pass urine;

  (d) the patient will be lying on a hard mattress on a plinth to facilitate resuscitation, should this become necessary. When the patient is awake and conscious, all this inevitably gives rise to a varying degree of discomfort.

7 Once the patient's condition is stable, he or she will be moved back to the ward, accompanied by the oxygen mask and drip feeds, as necessary.

    If the patient is comparatively young, he or she may be expected to recover fully and to resume normal life, making any discomfort or pain during the recovery process entirely acceptable. However, if the patient is an elderly person, other factors need to be considered, namely:

  (a) the patient's attitude to life, whether positive or negative;

  (b) whether the quality of the patient's life is already on the decline;

  (c) how long the patient has been suffering from pain and a curtailment of activity and mobility;

  (d) whether the patient has a marked fear of hospitals and an operation and would prefer to let nature take its course under prophylactic treatment—at home, if possible, or in hospital, if unavoidable;

  (e) prophylactic treatment, with antibiotics and pain killers, may well not offer the best hope of a cure, but it will avoid the more disturbing features of an operating programme as outlined above.

In general, before consenting on the patient's behalf to an operation, be sure that he or she has a genuine zest for life and will be content to suffer the stresses and struggles of 'maximum recovery' in order to have a better chance of survival, in preference to the alternative of prophylactic treatment. Also, before opting for an operation in the hope of prolonging the patient's life, make sure that your feelings are not selfish ones. You should try to put yourself in the patient's place, and choose what you believe would be his or her choice in the light of the considerations mentioned earlier.

LAVENDER CLARKE

FEAR

Let me not live to be a nuisance
To those with youth
Who strive to care.
Let me not live to feel
This moment,
Nor let them yet insist
That I survive.
For if I had a mind with which to speak it
Would I ever really want to stay alive?

DEIRDRE A. LEWIS

3

A Living Death

So death, the most terrifying of ills, is nothing to us, since so long as we exist, death is not with us; but when death comes, then we do not exist. It does not then concern either the living or the dead, since for the former it is not, and the latter are no more.

EPICURUS

Ask people what they would like to happen to them if they should have the misfortune to suffer from senile dementia and many of them say that they hope they will have the good luck to get a sharp attack of pneumonia—and that their doctor will not do anything foolish like trying to treat it. Or that someone will have the kindness to slip something into their tea. So why is it that the NHS spends a sizeable chunk of its budget trying to prolong the existence of patients suffering from senile dementia?

It is probable that most of those who suffer severely from it are unaware of their predicament, as they are unaware of practically everything else that makes human existence meaningful. The suffering falls chiefly on their nearest and dearest, contemplating the wreck of someone they once loved and knowing that before becoming demented, the victim would have given a great deal to secure an early and dignified end to his vegetoid existence were it possible.

What phrase shall we use to describe the fate of a man, a former cabinet minister, who suffered a very severe stroke several years ago? As well as paralysing him on one side he cannot speak, read, and write, although he is able to understand what is said to him.

There are two particularly cruel ironies about his present state. The first is that he used to be a brilliant communicator, making crisp and memorable speeches without notes. Now, his vocabulary is limited to three or four words which he cannot always use appropriately.

The second irony is that until his stroke, both he and his wife had been active members of the Voluntary Euthanasia Society, and his wife still is. It was an issue about which he felt strongly and I know exactly what he thought about the utter pointlessness, for him, of being kept alive in the sort of condition he now has to endure. From his answers to questions it is very evident that he would dearly like to be put out of his misery. He would willingly take a lethal overdose and it would be perfectly legal for him to do so, but for his family to place the necessary drugs on his bedside table would be a serious and imprisonable offence.

The courts are usually quite sympathetic in these situations ('. . . understand your feelings . . . no ulterior motive . . . quite accept that you loved him dearly . . . nevertheless court cannot ignore . . . two years probation') but they are unpredictable and sometimes feel the need to make an example.

There is a trend in several countries towards allowing patients a greater say in the timing and manner of their dying, but this is mainly evident in cases of terminal or rapidly progressive illness and it remains to be seen whether the trend has reached Westminster.

One of this man's frustrations is that his condition is evidently far from terminal. Like Karen Quinlan in America who remained nominally alive though cerebrally dead ten years after her life-support machines were switched off in the hope that she would follow suit—he could go on like this for years. Unlike Karen Quinlan, he knows that.

Although his condition is an emotional strain on his family, it is not a financial one. They are not short of money and he is being treated in an NHS geriatric unit with loving care.

His doctors are not even officiously trying to keep him alive. A few months ago, he had an attack of pneumonia and the doctors, with his enthusiastic approval, withheld antibiotics. (This is *passive* euthanasia and the practice is very widespread. Since in most cases the patients are in no position to say whether or not they wish to be treated, it is also decidedly *in*voluntary euthanasia.)

Here, then, lies the living body of a man who used to be one of this country's leading and most honoured citizens. Both before and since his stroke he has made it as clear as he possibly can that he does not wish to continue living like this.

In a generally free country, he is denied the one freedom that matters most to him at the moment: the freedom to obtain assistance in ending his life in dignity when he is no longer in a position to end it himself.

There are those who talk about the dangers of making such things legal, of the possibility of mistakes. Yet the freedom to make mistakes which mainly affect ourselves is one of the most basic freedoms of all. We permit it, in practice, to the sort of suicide whose death often causes great distress to others.

In an age when more people than ever live rather well, is it not strange that so many people have to die rather badly?

COLIN BREWER

THE TRAGIC CASE OF TONY BLAND

In April 1989 Tony Bland, a young Liverpool supporter from Keighley in Yorkshire, was severely crushed in the disaster at Hillsborough stadium. Dragged unconscious from the appalling carnage in which 95 people died, his oxygen-starved brain had been irreparably damaged and he has never regained consciousness. He now lies in deep coma in Airedale General Hospital, near Bradford. For three agonising years his parents, Allan and Barbara, have maintained their vigil at his bedside, but they realise there is no hope that their son will ever recover.

Able to breathe independently, Tony is not on a life support machine, but nevertheless he cannot feed himself and is only kept alive by an intravenous drip feed system. He could remain in this persistently vegetative state for another thirty years; meanwhile his parents suffer incalculable distress and there is considerable strain on the nursing staff who can do no more than maintain his condition.

Allan and Barbara have reached the difficult decision that they would prefer to let their son die, but the law will not allow them to withdraw the feeding tube, Tony's only hold on life. While it is permissible to switch off a ventilator, it is a criminal offence deliberately to deprive a living person of sustenance; the Blands risk a charge of manslaughter or even murder if they choose what most people would regard as the only merciful course of action.

This dreadful dilemma is exacerbated by the glare of publicity that has surrounded victims of the Hillsborough disaster. Tony's case is sadly not unique: at any one time about 1,500 people may be found in a similar state in British hospitals, but it is usually possible for feeding to be quietly withdrawn, bringing the patient a dignified death and the family a return to some semblance of normality. If Tony were to be allowed to die, everyone would know about it and the forces of law could not be seen to ignore what had happened: they would have no choice but to press charges.

No one would expect the Blands deliberately to incur further months of suffering after all they have endured. All they can hope for is a change in the law, so that they can at last let go and be left to grieve in peace.

THE NON-TERMINALLY ILL AND DISABLED

The Voluntary Euthanasia Society's principal object is still, I believe, 'to promote legislation which would allow an adult person, suffering from a severe illness for which no relief is known, to receive an immediate painless death if, and only if, that is their expressed wish.' Yet there is a tendency to echo the restriction of voluntary euthanasia as proposed in the Schwartzenberg Report (shortly to be debated by the European Parliament) to terminally ill patients.

The recommendation of that report that voluntary euthanasia be legalised for the terminally ill 'following the failure of palliative care correctly provided at both pyschological and medical level' would, if adopted and implemented, certainly be a great step forward in humanitarian medical practice. However, it does not go far enough, particularly in its restriction to terminally ill patients. This would disqualify, for instance, those suffering from total paralysis.

And a partial reform is often counter-productive, since it can delay far-reaching reforms for many decades.

Why, in fact, should the question of terminality be regarded as a relevant criterion at all? Indeed, provided pain is adequately controlled, the terminally ill patient is less likely to need euthanasia than someone whose equally distressing illness (or disability) is *not* terminal, since the latter could face many years of suffering. The two most important criteria are surely the intolerable nature of the condition and its incurability—the proper question being whether an intolerable condition is apparently incurable, not whether it is terminal.

As for the voluntary element, this is, of course, fundamental in the case of adult patients who are capable of communication, but in many other cases it cannot apply. These include cases where adults who would otherwise obviously be proper candidates for euthanasia have failed to provide an advance declaration asking for a quick, easy death for themselves in particular conditions.

There are also cases where scarce medical resources are wasted on human vegetables in whom the cerebral part of the brain is irreversibly dead. One stark instance of this was the case of the late Karen Quinlan, who, for ten years, from 1974, was obscenely kept 'alive' in an irreversible coma, in the USA—at a cost of millions of dollars and of considerable medical resources that could have benefited other patients.

That case is also tied up with the spurious ethical distinction between killing and letting die—between active and passive euthanasia. After the first year, it was decided to allow passive euthanasia by switching off the life-support system which, it was presumed, was keeping Karen 'alive'. But then her own heart and lungs took over, and as this was regarded as a supernatural miracle, it was decided that the treatment programme should continue, with rotas of nurses feeding this living corpse through the nose, pumping out excrement, turning the body, and massaging the limbs—though by this time the patient's brain had shrunk to the size of a golfball and it would certainly have been impossible for her ever to experience another thought.

A similar, more recent, American case was that of the late

Nancy Cruzan, whose equally pointless existence was finally brought to an end in December 1990, after six years; and the number of cases in the USA is said, at any one time, to be between 5,000 and 10,000.

This prevention of death not only ruins the lives of close friends and relatives: in Britain the drain on scarce hospital beds, nursing and other medical resources under the NHS is beginning to convince some of our politicians of the need to amend the law. However, they are wary of trying to legalise active euthanasia; they just want to establish the principle that withholding food in such circumstances is regarded as allowable passive euthanasia.

This is, of course, nothing but convenient casuistry, since it is obvious that to withhold food from a patient in *non*-euthanasia conditions would be murder. Thus, provided that no suffering is involved, it cannot possibly be the actual method of bringing about death that makes euthanasia moral, but the underlying incurable condition of the patient and the compassionate motive of the agent. And these are the criteria that we should stress—plus, where appropriate, the sustained voluntary factor. *Not* the terminal phase of the illness, which is completely irrelevant.

BARBARA SMOKER

THOUGHTS ON EUTHANASIA

Dean Inge, misnamed the gloomy, was asked whether there was any action which was always and altogether wrong, and he replied that 'mocking the insane' was absolutely evil. He added that there were not many examples of what is morally irredeemable, and of course he was right.

In most ethical issues, before we assess them as good or bad, and especially before we categorise behaviour patterns that emerge from these issues as right or wrong, we do well to introduce our decision with the words 'it all depends' for in most cases circumstances modify and even alter cases. For instance, is to inflict pain a good or bad thing to do? It all depends on who does it and why it is done. A doctor does the right thing if he inflicts pain on his patient in the process of trying to effect a cure. A hooligan does the wrong thing if he uses a doctor's scalpel to maim somebody in a drunken brawl.

Is it ever right positively to end a life? It all depends on what kind of life it is. It is surely not immoral to end the life of a garden flower at any time, or a poisonous snake, if found in the shoe you are about to put on. Even strict Buddhists, as I remember in Sri Lanka, when confronted with such snakes, corked them up in bottles and threw them into the bush.

What of human life? Are there any circumstances in which 'thou shalt not kill', either yourself or someone else, ceases to be an absolute prohibition and becomes 'situational'? Let us take suicide for example. One of my boyhood heroes was Captain Oates. As a member of the ill-fated Scott expedition to the Pole he found himself a deadly hindrance to the possible survival of his team mates because of his frost-bitten feet. With sublime self-sacrifice he said to Captain Scott, 'I'm going outside—I may be some time'. He left the snow-bound tent and never came back. He committed suicide and yet I believe he earned the accolade of his Lord, 'greater love hath no man than that a man should lay down his life for his friends.'

To kill oneself may be a sin, it is never a crime and can be the peak of unselfish goodness. This fact is recognised, or partially so, in the 1961 Act which removed suicide from the criminal code (but unfortunately leaves any individual of a second or third party vulnerable to penalties), and this brings me to another and more topical matter connected with this question of life and death. Has a human being a right to die? Or putting it more accurately, is it right for an individual to seek euthanasia, that is an easy or serene death?

I believe that sufferers in a terminal condition, accompanied by great pain and the breakdown of most of their normal faculties and controls, should be free to choose whether they wish to be kept physically ticking over by all the instrumentality of modern medicine, or whether the doctors and others should stop interfering with an inevitable process and confine their attention to making their passage into eternity as painless for them, and those at their bedside, as they can.

I am convinced that this choice is an inalienable right and is independent of any belief, or none, in the next world. For me death can be the entrance gate to eternal life, and that is why the church has so often said the most important thing about this life is to make a good death so as not to prejudice the future. What I do find peculiar is that many who profess their ardent desire to get to heaven take the most meticulous precautions to stay on earth.

Nonetheless to accept this right of voluntary euthanasia is far from simple in practice. Sufferers in a terminal condition may be quite incapable, when that condition is reached, of exercising such a right. Moreover, sufferers may believe that the condition is terminal when recovery is in fact possible. Therefore the declaration of intent to choose euthanasia must be made before the occasion for its carrying out is reached. Readers may know that in a Bill presented in the Lords in 1968, 30 days are prescribed as the required time between such a declaration and the emergency which called for its implementation.

Further, voluntary euthanasia requires the co-operation of nurses and doctors and this is indeed a thorny matter. I have no doubt that doctors do kill patients, in the sense of that word which means that they negatively allow sufferers to die by withholding therapy, or they hasten or produce a death situation by actively prescribing drugs which in the first instance relieve pain but are at the same time lethal. It is a cowardly reaction on the part of society to push the whole business under the medical carpet. We have no right to expose them to the hazards of breaking the law because the rest of us are not ready to take up our civic responsibility. I know how dangerous it is for parsons to be called upon to play 'God'. It is just as bad to ask the medical profession to exercise such a calling.

No one should under-rate the difficulties or the perils of voluntary euthanasia. One of them is highlighted by what I am convinced is a foolhardy enterprise in this field. To issue a kind of kit for would-be suicides, suggesting ways and means whereby they can effectively carry out their death wish, has no place in the considered philosophy of serene dying. It could be an open invitation to the mentally unstable and in any case would be like putting a bread knife into the hands of a child. This is no argument against bread knives but a solemn reminder that to use any instrument for any other purpose than that for which it is intended is perhaps another of the arguments with which I began.

As I understand it, the purpose of life is to love God and to enjoy Him forever. I believe that voluntary euthanasia can be a means to that end.

LORD SOPER

4

Personal Choice

If I can choose between a death of torture and one that is simple and easy, why should I not select the latter?

SENECA

When people talk of 'the fear of death', they often fail to distinguish between two types of fear which may be combined in experience but are separate in origin. One is the fear of the *state* of death (or non-existence); the other the fear of the *process* of dying, the agony of the transition to that state.

However, the division is not as clear-cut as that, because the two fears are interwoven. Mystics of all denominations have always claimed that a strong faith in after-life deprives not only the grave of its victory, but also death of its sting. Listen to Pope's 'Dying Christian to his Soul':

> Vital spark of heav'nly flame!
> Quit, oh quit this mortal frame:
> Trembling, hoping, ling'ring, flying,
> Oh the pain, the bliss of dying.

In other words, the mystic's faith can produce a form of euthanasia—a peaceful death of the body. The sceptic may call it a placebo-effect: it makes no difference. But now we come to the crucial point: this connection is reversible. If the agnostics among us could be assured of a gentle and easy way of dying, they would be much less afraid of *being* dead. This is not a logical attitude, but fear is not governed by logic. We tend to be guided by first impressions—of persons, landscapes, countries. An unknown country to which the only access leads through a torture chamber is frightening. And vice versa, the prospect of falling peacefully, blissfully asleep,

44

is not only soothing but can make it positively desirable to quit this pain-racked mortal frame and become un-born again. For after all, reason tells us—when not choked by panic—that before we were born we were all dead, and that our post-mortem condition is no more frightening than the pre-natal twilight. Only the process of transition, of *getting* un-born, makes cowards of us all. The whole concept of death as a condition would be more acceptable if dying would be less horrendous and squalid. Thus euthanasia is more than the administration of a lethal analgesic. It is a means of reconciling individuals with their destiny.

We are in dire need of such reconciliation and acceptance, for (apart from other obvious shortcomings) our species suffers from two severe biological handicaps imposed at the entry and exit gates of existence. Animals appear to give birth painlessly or with a minimum of discomfort. But owing to some quirk of evolution, the human foetus is too large for the birth-canal and its hazardous passage can entail protracted agony for the mother and—presumably—a traumatic experience for the new-born child. Hence we need midwives to aid us to be born. A similar situation prevails at the exit-gate. Animals in the wild, unless killed by a predator, seem to die peacefully and without fuss, from old age—I cannot remember a single description to the contrary by a naturalist, ethologist or explorer. The conclusion is inescapable: we need midwives to aid us to be unborn—or at least the assurance that such aid is available. Euthanasia, like obstetrics, is the natural corrective to a biological handicap.

ARTHUR KOESTLER

*   *   *

Arthur Koestler died on 3 March 1983. At the inquest the verdict was that he and his wife Cynthia killed themselves by taking an overdose of barbiturates. Mr Koestler was found seated in front of a window. Mrs Koestler was sitting on the settee. A half full glass of whisky and empty wine glasss containing the residue of a white powder were in the room. A jar of honey and an empty bottle of tablets were on the table.

In the words of the police spokesman, 'It was a scene of calmness'.

The following note, addressed 'To whom it may concern', was written and signed by Arthur Koestler in June 1982:

The purpose of this note is to make it unmistakably clear that I intend to commit suicide by taking an overdose of drugs without the knowledge or aid of any other person. The drugs have been legally obtained and hoarded over a considerable period.

Trying to commit suicide is a gamble the outcome of which will be known to the gambler only if the attempt fails, but not if it succeeds. Should this attempt fail and I survive it in a physically or mentally impaired state, in which I can no longer control what is done to me, or communicate my wishes, I hereby request that I be allowed to die in my own home and not be resuscitated or kept alive by artificial means. I further request that my wife, or physician, or any friend present, should invoke *habeas corpus* against any attempt to remove me forcibly from my house to hospital.

My reasons for deciding to put an end to my life are simple and compelling: Parkinson's disease and the slow-killing variety of leukemia (CCL). I kept the latter a secret even from intimate friends to save them distress. After a more or less steady physical decline over the last years, the process has now reached an acute state with added complications which make it advisable to seek self-deliverance now, before I become incapable of making the necessary arrangements.

I wish my friends to know that I am leaving their company in a peaceful frame of mind, with some timid hopes for a depersonalised after-life beyond due confines of space, time and matter and beyond the limits of our comprehension. This 'oceanic feeling' has often sustained me at difficult moments, and does so now, while I am writing this.

What makes it nevertheless hard to take this final step is the reflection of the pain it is bound to inflict on my few surviving friends, and above all my wife Cynthia. It is to her that I owe the relative peace and happiness that I enjoyed in the last period of my life—and never before.

Editor's note: The last paragraph explains the references in the press to 'a late decision' on the part of Cynthia Koestler. A further note setting out her reasons for the decision was found, but was not made public.

*   *   *

The note and letter below were sent to the Voluntary Euthanasia Society at the request of an 82-year-old member, a former teacher who died peacefully at the old people's home where she had been living for some years.

To whom it may concern
I have long realised that, at some later period, I would wish to end my life. I always hoped that it would become legal to seek help in this from my doctor; unfortunately it has not yet done so and I have had to act alone.

Please send a copy of my letter to the VES and another to my doctor.

Dear Relatives and Personal Friends,

You may know that I have long been a member of the Voluntary Euthanasia Society.

Today, with modern drugs and the emphasis on quantity of life rather than quality, there are many old people dragging out a mere existence, wanting to die but not being allowed to. I have seen and read enough to know that I personally fear this.

Surely it shows a lack of compassion not to help those who wish to go. Death is a natural sequence and in old age should be accepted, and suffering, where possible, be avoided. Of course, a lot depends on one's circumstances and on one's personal wishes. Many, no doubt, would still choose to continue as they do at present. *I am a great believer in freedom of choice*.

I have had a full, active and interesting life (with difficulties as well as compensations), including my retirement, and I know I have much to be thankful for, even now. But I know that I have passed my watershed (not the same age for everyone) and I am sure that my decision not to wait any longer is the right one. Particularly worrying is the contrast between my almost normal alertness in the mornings and my inability to do anything involving mental activity from the late afternoon onwards—even my confusion at times. Life, too, seems to have become purposeless. Relatives and friends are scattered or themselves have died. I am finding everything more difficult here, yet to move would not only be more difficult still but would serve no purpose. Merely to sit around and eke out a miserable existence— what a waste of resources!

I have always been a planner. When I planned to give up my home my motto was 'Better too soon than too late', and I have never regretted my decision. During the last few months I have felt rather as I did at that time— full of pleasant memories, but getting ready for a change.

I know that my death at this time will solve many problems, minor as well as major. But how much easier it would have been for everyone if I could have asked my doctor to call on her rounds, and how happy I should have been to see her pleasant face looking down at me as she gave me an injection and said good-bye. *I trust that the law will soon be changed so that older people, free from responsibilities, will have that freedom of choice. I even hope that my own action may help in some small way towards that end.*

*   *   *

The following letter was addressed to the writer's three sons and given to the Voluntary Euthanasia Society by one of them. He said, 'Would you like to use this? I feel that if she could have relied on help to die when she was ready to go, we'd have had her with us now. She wasn't ill.'

Dear

This is to say good-bye to you all and explain my reason for what I am going to do. You all know that for years I have always said I never intended to live to be very old. I have always dreaded the idea of old age, and especially after seeing what my parents went through. So, knowing I come of a long-lived family, it is up to me to do something about it. Do not imagine this is a sudden impulse, or that I am feeling miserable or depressed, quite the contrary. It is what I have been planning for a very long time, and now I feel the right time has come. I find it increasingly difficult to cope with things, and if I were to wait until I really could not manage without help, then I should have missed my opportunity, since it is obviously essential that there should be nobody around to interfere.

Anyway, I have lived for nearly three-quarters of a century, and that seems a very long time to me! Since I have nobody depending on me, I reckon I have a right to please myself.

You have all been good sons to me, and the only thing that worries me is the thought of upsetting you, but we all have to go some time, and it is so much better if one can do so without any suffering beforehand.

My love to you all,
Mum.

* * *

David was a very gentle, private and highly cultured man, tall, well-built and active. He was obviously well-educated but, so far as I know, possessed no academic qualifications. I suspect that in adolescence or early manhood he may have had some mental trauma which disqualified him from service in the War.

Shortly before the War he was given a home and taken into her household by a lady of independent means some thirty years his senior. Flora was a tremendous character, of a very generous and boisterous temperament, who enjoyed entertaining a large circle of friends. David helped on her fruit farm and as odd-job man about the house and was, for a man of his generation, amazingly proficient as cook, launderer, gardener and househusband. Flora had no children of her own, and their relationship appeared to be that of mother and son. David was devoted to her.

It was, I think, about 17 years ago, when David was 50 and Flora in her early eighties, that they moved to this area. They were very popular—Flora the life and soul of every company, David self-effacing but keeping the wheels turning.

I learnt from him early that Flora had no intention of declining into senility and that she had in their home the wherewithal to put an end to her life when she felt the time had come. As the years went by she became more and more crippled, though her mind was as active as ever. David did everything for her. With the inflation of the late '70s and early '80s they became quite badly off, and the necessities of life in this isolated part of the country are not cheap. She never asked for the medicine, but finally she lost her speech and her continence, and became in her nineties completely senile. For a matter of years rather than months David nursed her single-handed, never having more than two hours sleep at a stretch or more than half an hour out of the house to do the shopping.

Eventually, a year or two ago, Flora died a natural death in her own bed. After this David seemed to blossom. He could visit friends and walk to places he had not seen for years. He mowed the lawn for an octogenarian neighbour. He did the same for me when I was ill, and, when my wife was out, he would come across and make tea or coffee and bring it upstairs to me. He seemed to be in excellent physical and mental health. He told me he had no belief in a hereafter at all (though I advised him it might be prudent to keep an open mind on the subject) and when the time came he said he would have no hesitation in using the medicine that Flora had left untouched.

It came as a complete surprise to me when, in November, not having seen him about, I called and found him dead. He was in bed and had all the appearance of having died very peacefully. The house was spotless, the lawn was newly mown and there was a fine crop of vegetables in the garden ready for harvesting. Determined to the last to give the least possible trouble, he must have fasted for the last 24 hours, as the pathologist said the stomach was almost empty. I am sorry he did not say goodbye, but I can understand that he did not want any fuss or the risk of any argument about what he proposed to do. He had no relatives, of course, to distress.

I think he must have dreaded the possibility of a sudden stroke which might incapacitate him and leave him for years, perhaps, a helpless cabbage. Like me, he believed that nowadays, with medical care so obsessive and efficient, we owe a positive duty not to let ourselves become a burden. I admire enormously the courage he had to do such a thing while, so the doctor said, in excellent health; particularly when he was so sure there was nothing hereafter.

If there is a hereafter, David may have been a little perplexed at first and even supposed that his attempt had been unsuccessful, but I am sure he will have had no trouble with St Peter!

ANON.

AIDS AND DEATH

They say it's all too easy to make comments about how you want to end your life when you're fit and well, but for me the distant possibility of death has become a closer reality; for I have been given a 'terminal' diagnosis of AIDS. I choose to use the words 'life threatening' rather than 'terminal' because that gives me, along with others, hope, and reminds me that life itself is terminal.

I thought about my own death long before the onset of AIDS and tentatively made a decision that I wanted voluntary euthanasia, but four years into my diagnosis and seeing the death of many of my friends, thirty-six in all, I now know and believe I have made the right decision for me.

I've always been actively involved with the media, trying to educate people about HIV and AIDS and so when BBC television asked how I felt about appearing on their 'Family Matters' programme, I agreed, but this time I wasn't to speak about HIV and AIDS but about my decision to end my life. As we know a decision like this doesn't come easily, in fact it cannot be made in isolation, and so after lengthy discussion with my partner, family and friends it was agreed that when treatment has no more to offer, I'd take my life.

Although my family agreed with my decision there was still the problem of the law, so I stated that I would take my *own* life when the time came to avoid legal problems of 'aiding and abetting'. Having stated this on TV I phoned home to see if my parents were okay; it was then that a wonderful thing happened—both my parents and my partner agreed to be with me at the end.

A week or so later letters started arriving, and one in particular meant so much. A 79-year-old lady offered to be with me at the end, well aware that imprisonment was a distinct possibility. Next a family therapist stated she agreed with euthanasia and wanted to help. At work nurses and doctors felt a need to discuss the subject with me—it seemed what I had done was open the floodgates and health care workers now had permission without being made to feel unprofessional or guilty if they agreed with voluntary euthanasia.

Since the programme I have found that my job has changed to meet the demands of the people who attended the courses we run. We are now planning to devote an hour to the subject of voluntary euthanasia, for health care workers are willing to sit and discuss it and to look at exactly what is meant by the term 'a peaceful death'.

SHANE SNAPE

Editor's note: Shane Snape died in Spring 1992 from complications associated with AIDS. He was 32. He made a lasting contribution to improved care for those infected with HIV.

DO WE HAVE A DUTY TO DIE?

One of the more persistent objections one hears to the legalisation of voluntary euthanasia is that, once such an option were legitimate, people would come under various subtle, or even less subtle, forms of pressure or moral blackmail to take that option. Hence, even if it were still, in theory, the voluntary and informed decision of the patient, in practice many elderly prople who, in their heart of hearts, would prefer to go on living, however forlorn their lives, would succumb to what they perceived as the expectations of their family, or, even, of society at large. Thus, by imperceptible degrees, the right to die would become a duty to die.

Personally, I do not think that those who say it are just scaremongers. They may, indeed, underestimate the sheer stubbornness of old people who, in my experience at least, are not easily influenced to do anything they do not want to do but, doubtless, there would be some, perhaps more sensitive and conscientious than the rest, who, in these circumstances, would ask themselves whether it was not their duty to volunteer for euthanasia and equally, there would be those who were sufficiently unfeeling or unscrupulous to egg them on. Moreover, even if their own relatives were tactfully to refrain from dropping hints, the mere thought of becoming a burden to others, not to mention a drain upon society, would suffice to make them choose voluntary euthanasia as the only honourable course of action still open to them.

My own view would be that the premises on which the objection is based are plausible, what I would question is whether the argument constitutes an objection. So long as we are satisfied to regard death fatalistically, as just something that happens to us, as our ancestors have done since time immemorial, then, obviously, the question of a duty cannot arise. But once there is a choice, each of us has a responsibility for the choice we make. Hence, if we are in earnest in advocating medically assisted suicide, we can no longer evade the question as to where our duty lies.

Now, the most common reason for committing suicide is a purely negative one, namely that we have suffered enough already and refuse to submit to any further suffering. But most of our actions are multiply determined and there are usually other motives for suicide as well. Sometimes these are malign, as with certain aggrieved adolescents who may kill themselves in order to punish their uncaring parents. But sometimes they may also be altruistic: we may take our life in order that those we care about may live their lives more fully. The concept of a duty arises in connection with suicides of this nature. To seek oblivion because this is preferable to a painful existence is understandable and should arouse our compassion but it is not a moral gesture. On the other hand to commit suicide in order to liberate those on whom one is dependent is something that should surely earn our moral approbation. My answer would be, therefore, that if there *is* a duty to die it is one that arises from our basic human predicament, the fact that we are dependent on others, and it is a duty we owe to those we cherish.

Well, if you have patiently borne with me so far, you may, perhaps, be thinking that while all this sounds logical enough, it is indelicate on my part to be discussing such matters. Death, you may protest, has terrors enough for all of us without my adding to our anxieties by insinuating that we may be failing in our duty by just continuing to exist! If I were a young man I think I would have to plead guilty to a lack of tact in taking this line, for, how can the young understand the feelings of those for whom death is no longer a comfortably remote contingency? But I am a man pushing seventy and, although at the moment I am in excellent health, the thought of death can never be very far from my consciousness. I therefore feel that I need make no apology for discussing these issues in a cool and detached way.

My own attitude has been strongly coloured by the fact that, in the course of my life, I have known so many women whose lives were devastated by having to take care of a helpless elderly parent or spouse. And, of course, I have read about, or heard about, many more whom I did not know personally. Presumably such a fate may also befall a man, but women, in our society, are much more vulnerable to the social pressures and moral blackmail that can make such demands. I do not suppose my own experience in this regard can be so very different from others, but it has made me determined never to become a burden on my wife, let alone on my daughter, and I have solemnly vowed to myself to do what is necessary to this end. Proponents of the welfare state may object, at this point, that, in a properly run country, it should never be necessary for anyone to become a burden on anyone else. That, if one does become decrepit, one ought to be properly cared for by trained professionals at the public expense. But, I ask you, is such a utopian solution realistic? The actual choice I would have to make today, if I wanted to spare my wife, would be to enter a nursing home for as long as my savings lasted or, if I could not afford to do so, seek a place in some state-run geriatric institution if such were available. But even if my immediate physical needs were then catered for by professionals, my wife would still have to endure the anguish of watching me as I become progressively more helpless and debilitated.

I am sometimes asked by those who know that I believe in the right to die with dignity how one is to tell when the hour has come. This is indeed a tricky question because dying is a gradual business. Moreover, nature has so contrived matters that, at each stage, we adjust to our condition which then no longer seems as fearful or degrading as it did previously. This is, no doubt, a mercy and, indeed, those whose duty it is to look after geriatric patients dwell on this fact and point out that however decrepit or handicapped the patient, they become reconciled to their lot and manage somehow to enjoy themselves as best they can. Whether this is so, or how often this is so, it is an argument that is often brought against voluntary euthanasia. On the other hand, it is not an argument that can carry much weight with those who believe in the right to die with dignity, which is incompatible with extreme disability and still more perhaps with senility. We would literally rather be dead than live on as contented cabbages. The danger we dread is that we might slip into senility, or senile dementia, by degrees without realising what has happened to us—as, I gather, is liable to happen to victims of Alzheimer's disease. Some people have even gone so far, in order to forestall such a fate, as to make a compact with a trusted friend whereby each would be obliged to tell the other when the time had come to take evasive action. Whether this actually works in practice, knowing the frailties of human beings, I have yet to hear.

At all events, I have given the matter some thought and I have decided that there are three main contingencies as a result of which I would not want to go on living. They are (1), if I were facing a complete loss of memory, (2), if I could no longer control my bladder and bowels and (3), if I were no longer able to feed myself or perhaps even if I could no longer enjoy my food. I put memory first because if we lose our long-term memory we have, in effect, lost our sense of identity, we are no longer the person we once were, while, if we lose our short-term memory, we are incapable of learning anything new. For example, we would read the headline in today's paper and the next minute be oblivious of ever having done so. Since one of those things that keep us going is our desire to know what will happen next, our life would have come to a stop in any meaningful sense; consciousness would have shrunk to a point; our body alone would persist. Incontinence is peculiarly horrifying, partly because of its anti-social implications and partly because it represents such a cruel reversion to infancy. Having to be fed is not, perhaps quite so disgusting but it, too, spells a regression to infancy and is a constant reminder of our utter helplessness. I should perhaps have added a fourth contingency, that of being in agonising and intractable pain with no prospect of relief. The proponents of the hospice movement, and the anti-euthanasia lobby in general, insist that the problem of pain is already largely under control and that we are on the verge of conquering it altogether. I wish that were so but I think such a claim should not go unchallenged. It would not sound very convincing to some of the victims of arthritis that I have known to tell them that chronic pain is a thing of the past.

I have tried to make explicit the circumstances in which I would feel justified in taking my own life. Those who condemn suicide, and there are many, sometimes denounce it as being 'the coward's way out'. But, while a reasonable amount of stoicism in the face of adversity is to be admired, I can see nothing glorious in suffering for its own sake when it has become hopeless. At the same time I would like to think that there was more to my suicide than simply avoidance of suffering. I would be happy if my loved ones believed that at least part of my motive for ending my life was to improve the quality of *their* lives, by removing from their midst the dreadful encumbrance of my own ailing body. At all events, it was such thoughts as these that prompted the reflection that dying may not be merely a right but also, on occasion, a duty.

JOHN BELOFF

SUICIDE: THE RIGHT AND THE DILEMMA

Moral views about suicide have changed in our century at least as radically as about sex. In the Notebooks that Ludwig Wittgenstein kept during the First World War, he wrote, 'If suicide is allowed then everything is allowed. If anything is not allowed then suicide is not allowed. This throws a light on the nature of ethics, for suicide is, so to speak, the elementary sin.' But here, the outlook of our grandparents seems very remote. The 1961 Suicide Act, removing the legal prohibition, did not arouse the opposition run into by other liberalising laws of the Sixties. And few now think that suicide calls for moral condemnation.

Even now, news of a suicide can give us a greater sense of shock than when we hear of a natural death, but we no longer rationalise this as an awareness of moral wrongdoing. Our responses vary according to cases. Where the suicide is of someone suffering from severe depression or other mental disturbance, we see it as a product of the illness, and so we are reluctant to hold the person responsible. When we hear that Arthur Koestler has decided to end his life rather than face further illness and decline in old age, and that his wife has chosen to go with him, we have no difficulty in seeing how this decision could be perfectly rational. Who, in such a case, is in a position to say they made the wrong choice?

It may seem there is nothing to say about the morality of suicide. In the case of the disturbed person not responsible for his acts, moral criticism does not arise. And, in other cases, surely people have a right to decide for themselves whether to go on living? In general, the change in attitudes is surely an improvement. In the past, the victims of moral disapproval were either those whose suicide attempts had failed, or the families of successful attempts, who were made to feel that the death was somehow disgraceful. It is obvious that the last way to help either of these groups is by moralising after the event. The decline in this is an unqualified good.

But it does not follow that there are no problems about whether an act of suicide is right. Where someone thinking of suicide is sufficiently in control to deliberate about it, there are questions to consider about the rationality of the act and about its morality.

The question about rationality is easier to state than sometimes to answer. Would the person's future life be worth living? In the case of a progressively worsening illness, a stable view may sometimes not be hard to arrive at. But, where you are being driven to suicide by losing your job, or your husband's desertion, or by mounting debts, the matter may be less clear. Most of us are bad at predicting how likely things are to improve. And suicide cannot be justified without comparing it with less drastic steps. Someone who would not usually even consider leaving his family, changing his job, emigrating or seeking psychiatric help is unwise to rule out such steps when he enters the region where he does not rule out suicide. It is worth talking to others, whether friends or the Samaritans, who may provide a different perspective. And because moods are so fluctuating, it is hard to be sure that any suicide decision is rational unless it is adhered to for a fairly long time.

The moral question is about the effect of suicide on others. Some people may have lives (perhaps with severe and incurable mental disorders, or involving great pain) where their interests should come before any loss to others. But sometimes an act of suicide, particularly at the vulnerable student stage of life, can shatter the lives of parents and family to a degree the person would not have guessed. And someone who is old or ill, and fears being a burden, should not assume that suicide will help others. Our psychology is not so simple. Shock, grief and guilt can be a far greater burden.

We are halfway towards the right climate of opinion on suicide. We have moved away from legal penalties and from insensitive condemnation. We no longer think suicide a blasphemous interference with a divine plan, and prefer to think that people have a right to dispose of their own lives. But cases vary, and some rights need to be exercised with gentleness and consideration for others.

JONATHAN GLOVER

5

Acts of Compassion

Si je ne suis plus en état d'aider le malade à vivre, je dois l'aider à mourir.

AXEL MUNTHE

My husband killed himself a few weeks ago. I hope that some of the people, especially MPs, who are so opposed to any consideration of legalising euthanasia will read this, and other more eloquent accounts of why and how this happens, and think again. Please.

He wasn't young—late 60s—and had been diagnosed as suffering from multiple sclerosis about ten years ago. Until then he had had perfect health. From the early days of the diagnosis we agreed that suicide might eventually be the only escape route if his life threatened to become intolerable through total or near-total immobility. We both had, I have, strong moral convictions, which include the notion that one human right should be the right to decide to end one's life.

The first years weren't bad, but in the last two he deteriorated a lot and became virtually house-bound, though still able to get about the house and to climb, laboriously, upstairs. Music and books remained the stimulus and solace they had always been. But about two months ago he got much worse and was no longer able to stand, or to turn over in bed without help. Blurred vision began.

The NHS were magnificent—district nurses visiting daily, equipment loaned, frequent visits by a caring doctor. I don't think we could have had better or more committed care if we had been able to put thousands of pounds on the table. But. It took about 15 minutes to help him from the bed hastily installed downstairs onto a wheelchair, then I wheeled him into the sitting room, then the tiring hoisting and heaving to get him onto a chair. Suppositories, commode, inspection for bed sores, constant fatigue, and the conviction that life as he knew it and defined it was finished. J (we'll call him that) had always said that life wasn't life without some control over your body, and now he could scarcely sit in a chair without slipping down. Enough was enough—to him, this would be an existence of physical humiliation, totally restricted activity and perhaps the prospect of life in hospital. He didn't want it, and I agreed. Yes, of course I admire the courage of those who go on, but J's courage was of a different sort.

We discussed it fully. His means of ending his life were of course very limited, but he had already decided on the course to take. He was very calm, cheerful too, in the last couple of days, and we talked a lot. He was absolutely determined. And I knew that for him *this was the right choice*. One little example—'I'll never take a book from a top shelf of a bookcase again,' he said. But he spoke too of the pressure on an overworked and underfunded health service, and the fact that his days as a productive member of society were over. So those last days aren't a tragic or distressing memory. Not at all. But he stopped watching TV news or reading newspapers.

The first attempt failed—he fell asleep too soon. In the morning he said, 'But of course I will try again.' Then I realised that I wanted to help him—not to lie tense and sleepless upstairs, wondering. This was what he desperately wanted—a lonesome journey, but less so if someone is there at the end.

So this is how it was. We were both relaxed and calm and we talked for hours on the last day. Then the slow progress to bed. I didn't feel like crying except when he asked me to wash his feet. He didn't want them to be dirty when authority took over. But I didn't cry; it was too important and too charged with different emotions for that.

He made the preparations. Then he took the sedatives and said: 'It's marvellous that you're here. Make sure I'm dead before you call anyone. I'm really glad to be leaving, though I'll miss you.' The sedatives worked. He died quickly, very quickly, and the sense I had was of total peace. His hands lay on his chest, and I sat with him for hours, literally for hours.

Just after he died there seemed to be the slamming of a door, and a faint roll of thunder. There was nothing to be frightened by. I was so glad that I had shared and helped—how could I ever have thought (as I had) that I must not be involved.

I perjured myself at the inquest—I couldn't face going public, and this is the only part of it I feel ashamed of. I couldn't face the hassle. And I am angry, very angry, that I had to tell lies and even more angry that J had to act so furtively, with support only from me, none from society, in this decision.

Were we wrong? I don't think so. Now there is a dull ache, but no regret—I'm glad he has escaped.

ANON.

*　　*　　*

In 1939 my mother was dying—she had been ill off and on for many years—this time she had only a couple of weeks at the most and the end would be sticky and very distressing for her two sisters. The doctor—a young man from London down for health reasons—talked to her and explained things—and offered her euthanasia—told her to talk it over with her brother and sister (I was away in the country). She decided for it.

The night he was coming she demanded a slap-up dinner with wine—ours was a teetotal household—wrote me a letter and said goodbye. So she died with dignity—thanks to this young doctor.

I only hope I have the chance to do the same.

VALDA GRIEVE

*　　*　　*

My mother was a great character, lively, opinionated, quick-witted, and, when she celebrated her 85th birthday, still the Queen Bee taking the centre of the stage. I found it difficult to imagine life without her.

But she had been ailing for some months, and fiercely resented the slightest ill-health. She would say that her time had come and she was looking forward to the big sleep that could not be far away. I said firmly that I still needed her.

Soon after her birthday she had a stroke and became paralysed on one side. At first her mind remained alert. She was determined to go into hospital, and I now feel sure that this was to make it easier for me to carry on with my work. But her mind was gradually narrowing to two themes, hospital and sleeping pills. She had always taken these at night, and now she wanted them by day. If I tried to keep her off them she would try to struggle out of bed to get at them. 'You said you wouldn't let me suffer,' she would say.

Finally she went into a hospital room, and immediately her mind gave out. Perhaps she had had another stroke. Now there were two things in her life—she could squeeze my hand and nod when I talked to her, and she could say, 'Bring my sleeping pills.' This soon degenerated into 'slippers'. 'Quick, darling; hurry, sleepers, quick.' This was her sole remaining idea.

I have heard of people becoming cheerful idiots, but she was not cheerful. In her confusion (judged to be irreversible) she was distressed, frantic, unsmiling, desperate, bewildered. To leave her by herself was heartrending. I fed her barbituates dissolved in brandy, squirting it to the back of her mouth using a plastic syringe. But she kept waking up to this mockery of life. Her heart was strong. I read in the nurse's notes, 'Urine offensive, speech incoherent.' At that moment I decided that my Queen Bee mother was not going to linger on in this bedlam state. I had to rescue her from the nightmare, even if I ended up in a prison cell. So I told her I loved her and was sending her to join my father. This time I gave her all the remaining capsules and she was very soon delivered from her bondage.

It is true that I was delivered at the same time, and if rewards are ever given, the women who care year after year for demented parents may deserve a greater reward, though I see no merit in avoidable martyrdom when the suffering involves the patient as well as the carer. But of course things were relatively easy for me; my mother was quite old, I knew her own wishes very clearly, and I had the means.

So I have no regrets and would do the same thing again.

And if I were to suffer a stroke as she did, I hope that someone would do the same for me. It would be safer to leave me mouldering in a hospital ward, but it would not be kinder. If I had let my mother live on, I should have had it on my conscience for ever.

ANON.

* * *

My experience may be of help to other people faced with a similar situation. There are two issues: the need to alert younger people to the problems they may eventually have to face, and the position of people who are asked to help another person to die. It is the latter that chiefly concerns me here.

Eighteen months ago my wife was dying of cancer, fortunately here at home, with myself as sole nurse—except, towards the end, for help from our excellent district nurses (interestingly, they did not, really, approve of euthanasia). My wife knew she was dying, quite calmly; and when she got so weak she could not even turn over in bed without my help, she said she had, thank you, had enough. She meant it—and one knows when someone means it. My medical helpers (and, before and after, I've found the medical profession solidly on my side) must be protected at all costs, so I shall give no details of what happened. But I got a fatal dose, told my wife what I should be doing, and we had an hour or so in which to say goodbye—a huge privilege. The death was slow, and there was the fear, fortunately ill grounded, that I had not given her enough.

I was extremely lucky to have everything in my own hands. But even then my position was difficult. What would be lethal? And how to get it? How protect whoever told me, and provided the stuff? And (least important of all, but one might as well be careful even though in those circumstances one's own living or dying is a matter of indifference) how protect oneself?

All these questions will be suddenly upon anyone who finds themselves in my position, and at a moment probably when they are in the nature of the case already doing five jobs at once.

I should mention that, for my part, I am only certain what it is right for one to do in such a case if one profoundly loves the dying person and is close enough to them to have more right to help them than anyone else has.

As to the other matter I mentioned, alerting younger people to their future needs—I talk about this to people of all ages, especially in connection with my own death. Perhaps the first thing is the simple task of getting them to realise that each one of us is going to die. Accept that, with a ripe gladness, and the rest follows.

Anon.

COMPASSION ON TRIAL

Sylvia Williams was a woman with a zest for life. Active and fun-loving, she was strong and fit and liked to get her own way. When, at the age of 48, she was diagnosed as having motor neurone disease, she and her whole family were devastated. This progressive condition slowly destroys the nervous system, causing paralysis of the muscles but leaving the brain unaffected. There is no known cure.

Mrs Williams was determined not to be beaten by the disease. Her doctor prescribed medicine to relieve the symptoms, including sleeping pills, and she bought herself a rowing machine to keep her muscles exercised. In the end, however, she began to lose the battle. It became more and more difficult to move her legs and arms, her voice deteriorated and even breathing became difficult. Over the months she became very lonely, unable to face going out and meeting people with whom she could no longer hold a conversation.

Throughout the course of her illness she had had the support of her four daughters, and when, by Christmas 1988, she could no longer manage on her own, her eldest daughter Phillipa Monaghan left her home in London and moved into her mother's flat to care for her. She and her mother had always been particularly devoted to each other; it caused Phillipa great anguish to watch the slow deterioration of the woman she loved and relied on.

The previous summer, Mrs Williams had begun talking of

taking her own life. Above all, she dreaded ending her days in hospital, at the mercy of other people. From time to time she raised the subject again, but as the months went by and her condition worsened she was no longer physically capable of taking any action herself. She then besought her daughters for help, appealing to them to help her die, and in February 1989 she began to organise her funeral arrangements. By the end of the month it was obvious that she had little time to live. Her daughters gathered round and the doctor talked of admitting her to hospital. Clearly she felt that she must persuade someone to help her carry out her wishes without further delay.

It was on Phillipa that the full force of her appeals fell. Over several days she must have willed herself to do as her mother asked, and on 16 March she took the plunge. Mixing about 60 tablets with bananas and milk, she tried to feed the cocktail to her mother, but the sick woman could no longer easily swallow and began choking. In desperation Phillipa pulled a plastic bag over her mother's head and put a pillow on top. By the time her sisters returned to the flat their mother was dead.

The following day Phillipa went to the police and described how her mother had planned her own death and how she herself had carried out her wishes. 'I didn't want my mum to die,' she said, 'I wanted her to stop suffering.' The police had no choice but to charge the distraught young woman with attempted murder, but at her trial a compassionate judge released her on two years' probation, deeming that she had been put under great emotional pressure and had already suffered enough.

Insofar as Mrs Williams had openly exercised her right to dictate her own death, justice had been done, but at what cost to the woman who, terrified and unskilled, had to try to grant her wish?

*   *   *

On 5 July 1990 a Leicester brother and sister, Andrew and Nicola Thompson, aged 25 and 21, appeared in court charged with the attempted murder of their mother, 59-year-old Mrs Pauline Barbor, who was in hospital with terminal cancer.

They were granted bail on condition that they made no further attempt to see their mother, surrendered their passports (they both worked in Spain) and reported daily to the police. Subsequently an application to a High Court Judge allowed them one more visit to their mother before her death on 15 July.

Pauline Barbor had known for eighteen months that she was suffering from breast cancer. She had undergone operations and chemotherapy treatment, all in vain, and when she was admitted to hospital Andrew and Nicola came back to Leicester to be with her. Towards the end they were in the agonising situation of watching her deterioration and unbearable pain, knowing that she had frequently expressed her wish to be relieved of her suffering and to be helped to die. They had talked of this before going to the hospital on 3 July and had decided that, given the courage, they would try to grant her wish. Taking a motorised syringe containing the pain-controlling drug diamorphine, Andrew administered the whole contents, then he and his sister sat holding thier mother's hands and trying to comfort her.

In the event their attempt failed. Nursing staff at the hospital, realising that Mrs Barbor had received a whole day's dosage of diamorphine, gave her an antidote which prolonged her life for twelve more days.

Andrew and Nicola made no attempt to conceal their intervention. Their sole concern was for the welfare of their mother and they told police that they had decided to take her life because of the severe pain she was in; they wanted to end her life to avoid a painful and lingering death.

The ordeal of these two brave young people was far from over. On the day of their mother's funeral they were again in court, and they had to endure a further four harrowing months, grieving for their mother and dreading their trial, before their case came up at Leicester Crown Court in November. They pleaded guilty and were treated leniently by the judge who told them, 'I am sure that the stress of seeing your mother suffering was overwhelming for you. I accept that she pleaded with you to end her suffering and I also find that you deliberated long before deciding to embrace the course you did.'

Andrew and Nicola were granted a 12-month conditional discharge and, amid tears of relief, spoke of their gratitude to the judge for his understanding. They still, however, maintain their view that terminally ill patients have the right to die, and their aim in seeking maximum publicity for their case was to highlight this injustice and to try to save other relatives from having to go through the same ordeal. Shortly after their discharge, their story was told in a documentary on ITV, and on 'The Time, the Place' the following morning, 24,000 viewers phoned in to express their sympathy and support.

*   *   *

Anita Harding was born in 1900. She lost both parents when she was six years old and, having no other relatives, was brought up in a charitable boarding school. After leaving school she worked in a library, interested herself in travel, public affairs, painting and the arts, and was known for her beautiful needlework, some of which was shown at an exhibition at Hever Castle. During the war, she went into the Civil Service, where she remained until her retirement.

By 1978, when she joined the Voluntary Euthanasia Society, she had been forced by increasing blindness to move out of her home and live in sheltered accommodation.

By 1983, Anita Harding had good grounds for wishing to bring her life to a close. Her age was 84, and her physical condition was very poor. She was arthritic, with chronic back pain. She had difficulty in breathing. She was almost blind and would soon have become totally blind; and she was very deaf. She had no family, her few friends had died before her and she was dependent on the kindness of voluntary helpers whenever she needed to leave her one-room flat. Always somewhat withdrawn, she suffered from bitter loneliness, and when she found that her hearing was rapidly deteriorating still further, she realised that her isolation would soon be complete. Her life had become an intolerable burden.

At such an age and in such circumstances, surely she had the moral right to choose to die. She also had the legal right. But she was uncertain whether she would be able to claim her right alone, and begged for the comfort of a friend to hold her hand as she lost consciousness for the last time, and to make sure that she did not return to the same intolerable life made worse by the brain or liver damage that might result from the attempt.

When Mrs Charlotte Hough, a voluntary helper who had become a friend, promised that she would not allow Miss Harding to regain consciousness—so enabling her to die with an easy mind—she thought she would only have to sit beside her as she died. But the drugs Miss Harding had taken, though leading to rapid unconsciousness, did not result in a speedy death. So Mrs Hough, faced with the dilemma of breaking her promise or breaking the law, placed a plastic bag over Miss Harding's head while she was in a coma. Because of the uncertainty as to whether the death was caused by the bag or by the barbiturates Miss Harding had taken, the original charge of murder was reduced to attempted murder, to which Mrs Hough pleaded guilty. She was sentenced to nine months' imprisonment. Her appeal was refused.

*   *   *

A harsh sentence of life imprisonment was imposed on Anthony Cocker for the murder of his wife in January 1988. At the trial at Manchester Crown Court Mr Justice Boreham refused to allow the jury to consider the defence of manslaughter by reason of provocation, a refusal that so incensed the jury that they wrote a letter of protest—an almost unheard-of occurrence.

Anthony Cocker's wife suffered from Friedrich's Ataxia, an incurable condition with effects similar to those of multiple sclerosis. She had seen her sister die of it in institutional care and dreaded her own coming end. The disease confined her to a wheelchair and made her incontinent, and the whole burden of nursing was borne by her husband, who also had to suffer the strain of her increasing irritability and sleeplessness, and her frequent demands that he should end her life. It was on being woken by these demands after a disturbed night that his control finally snapped and he first strangled, then smothered her.

Thankfully for Anthony Cocker, the public took a kinder

view than that of the judge. He was overwhelmed with letters of support, and even visited in prison by a woman who subsequently became his wife. Meanwhile a Local Review led to a ruling by the Parole Board that he should be transferred to an open prison and he was finally released in May 1992. A fund was set up to help him on his release, for he had meanwhile lost the home he had shared with his first wife since it was specially adapted accommodation and was needed for another disabled person.

Anthony Cocker will, with help, be able to pick up the threads of his life again. But will he ever be able to forget the ordeal of an outrageous punishment meted out after years of suffering and devoted care?

I WAS WITH HER WHILE SHE DIED

A wonderful thing happened to me a little while ago that I think everyone ought to know about, because it holds out such hope to us all and meant so much to me.

My first wife and I had broken up decades ago, but of course remained friends. Returned from a short job abroad and aware that she was seriously ill, I arranged to travel up to see her, in a few days' time. On the appointed day she rang me up and said: 'Do you think you could stay the night? I desperately need your help.' 'Desperately' was not a word she would ever normally use.

Reaching her house I found she was still able, just, to get about and had indeed managed to put some lunch for us on the table. But in the last month or so she had lost two stone in weight and she was, clearly, dying of cancer. It took me a minute to realise what she wanted me for. And as she saw that I *had* realised it, ten years dropped from her face, she became debonair, almost gay. 'My good angel sent you! I am so happy—no, joyful!'

It appeared that she had long since thought out her suicide, and prepared the means; but for weeks she had been lying awake at night turning over the details of the act, to make sure all the links were sound. She needed someone by her to ensure that nothing went wrong; and who would if necessary complete the act himself. Then she could relax, and *enjoy* her dying.

She said she had reached a good age—she was in her 80s—had had a most fulfilling life, had lost nearly all her friends as they aged, had nothing particular that she still wanted to do, and was damned if she could, if she could help it, allow herself a long, miserable drawn-out end, being—she said—a nuisance to everyone and (with a grin) a charge on the NHS. Death itself she had—as I have too—always felt beside her as a good friend: no enemy. And the change-over from life to death she had very positive ideas about: individual ones of her own, but formed against the background of the Church of England, which she had been brought up in and had now, in a sociable way, returned to. (She had left suggestions about her funeral service for her Vicar.)

Through lunch and on until evening, when she was ready for her early bed, we had a marvellous time: going over early days, laughing a great deal (as one can, from the detached position of age), and simply enjoying each other's existence. And she was more open than I have, I think, ever known her: telling me things about herself many of which were new to me. 'I am happy, so happy—I could dance!' 'What an adventure!' She had not only accepted death but was looking forward to it, almost was impatient for it: as a thing of grandeur, sweetness. Space.

About eight o'clock she went upstairs, washed, put on her best nightdress, and lay down on her bed, the pills (I've forgotten what they were) beside her. After a while she shovelled up the pills, as if they were sweeties (which made us laugh) and lay back, eyes shut, on the pillow. 'This is bliss. All my troubles dropping away.' Her face was entirely serene. Sitting by the bed, I held her hand.

And that was that. Twice there was a slight intake of breath; and once her hand in mine suddenly tightened—that was perhaps the moment when she died. Otherwise nothing. Throughout, her face was completely serene. When I was sure she must be dead I tidied her hair. Then I spent the night in the next room, sleeping a bit, and going in from time to time (one needs the body to be there) to be with her, touch her hand, kiss her forehead.

Next day the relations, not at my instigation—I had wanted to leave things as they were—removed the signs of euthanasia and concocted a story (which I had then, against the grain, to help spread) that she had been found dead in her sleep; and the doctor, bless him, signed a fictitious death certificate. The relatives felt that some of her acquaintances, as distinct from her friends—who were told the truth—might be shocked and hurt if they knew the true story. Also, maybe, they wanted to protect me. Sheer conventionality may also have come into it.

The law would have required me to refuse, to betray, my old friend, once wife. And she might then have dragged on for another stretch in the wretched existence she had so resolutely taken steps to avoid. What a law!

Think too of the beauty, joy, the sweetness of her death. The loving time we had together. The fulfilment for me: our relationship brought thus full cycle. The honour she did me. And finally this: of all the people close to me who have died, she alone has left me with no feeling of regret. Her death was a completion. Was right. The books are sweetly closed. May each one of us be able to die as well.

ANON.

A DUTCH EXPERIENCE OF DEATH

My wife died about five months ago. She suffered from an inoperable malignant tumor in the pancreas. She had been ill for eight months and I had the privilege of caring for her by myself at home.

The best part our marriage of 38 years was the last two months: we both knew then that her death was irrevocable. And this period of facing not death but the end of her life has brought us closer together than anything before ever did. We talked about memories of the past, but mostly about the future for the children and for me.

We together prepared her cremation, visitors to invite, music to be played, speakers (she wanted me to be the only one, which I promised).

I asked her, in that period, whether she was afraid of death and she answered full-heartedly: 'No, not at all; I only fear much pain, but there will be no pain in dying as the doctor has promised.'

At a certain moment she asked me: 'But who will you take with you to buy a new pair of trousers?' We smiled together. But her underlying question I can answer in all sincerity by saying that these two months of living intensely together have certainly given me the mental strength to go on with life without her. She is forever inside me; I still feel part of her 'warmth' and this helps me in my relationships with other people. In fact it is this warmth that makes me feel strong enough and even glad to tell you about all this.

And I realise that these two months of 'happiness' were possible also, because we both were aware that the end of her life would be a good one, fully conscious and without pain.

And the end of her life was indeed perfect. Arrangements had been made in our home for giving an adjustable supply of morphine. After every one of the children had talked with her or sat simply by her bedside, the morphine supply was increased. I then sat by her side, took her hand and we talked softly. Gradually she fell asleep; her last words to me were: 'I feel so very happy now.' And this showed clearly on her face in her last sleep, finally completely without pain and fully satisfied.

When I returned to the family there was no great grief or sadness in us, because we all had had the time to be with her so very intensely.

And even now, five months after her death, we still feel no great pain or grief. Of course I miss her every day and so do the children, but somehow we feel much closer together than we ever did before; somehow she has awakened a kind of 'warmth' in us which we have never before known so clearly and about which we feel very happy.

Probably the eight months of caring for her and especially the last two months of being extremely close together and the ending of her life together, have helped me to go through the most difficult part of the mourning process. And this gives me a feeling of gratitude instead of insurmountable grief.

On the basis of this experience, I am convinced that this is the only way one should leave life if possible.

MAX DE LANGE

IN MEMORY OF AN AFGHAN HOUND

His sign was gracefulness. His silver coat
flowed in the wind created by his speed.
Age made him grey and slow until he could
no longer stand. My needle found his vein
and with a look as if of gratitude
he slowly wagged his tail and fell asleep.
Whom should I ask to work this act of grace
on me, a human, when the time will come?

ERIC VIO

6

The Doctors' Dilemma

In our times, the physicians make a kind of scruple and religion to stay with the patient after he is given up; whereas in my judgement, if they would not be wanting to their office, and indeed to humanity, they ought both to acquire the skill and to bestow the attention whereby the dying may pass more easily and quietly out of life.

The Advancement of Learning. FRANCIS BACON

When the Voluntary Euthanasia Society was established in 1935, its founders included a physician, Dr Millard, and the royal surgeon, Lord Moynihan. Admittedly, the society currently lacks a surgical or even a medical peer, but its members include several non-medical ones and quite a few doctors who are not peers. Yet doctors on the whole seem reluctant to debate voluntary euthanasia, although, according to many opinion polls, a large majority of patients want legislation.

The usual arguments against legalisation are variations on one basic theme: doctors should not play at being God. This is rather like saying that doctors shouldn't interfere with nature, which is something that most of us do several dozen times a day.

We like to think that most of this interference is beneficial, but some of it is not, notably the keeping alive of patients who would rather be dead and who in less medically sophisticated times often would have been.

Ironically, a great deal of *involuntary* euthanasia goes on every day. Who has not encountered the following situation many times? A patient with dementia, or a severe stroke, or advanced cancer develops pneumonia. The decision has to be made: to treat or not to treat?

Often the decision is fudged but often the outcome is that

the pneumonia is not treated because those in charge—ordinary doctors and nurses—believe (although they do not usually say as much), that it would be best for such patients if they did not live.

Evidently, it is acceptable to end the lives of selected patients in this inefficient way, often without ascertaining the views of the patient or his family. It is evidently not acceptable to end their lives in a more humane and predictable way, even if the patient has expressed a clear preference for death or has appointed trusted friends or relations to speak for him in this matter.

This sort of casuistry may have been all right for mediaeval doctors of theology. It will not do for modern doctors of medicine.

Those who fear 'abuses' if voluntary euthanasia were legalised should ask themselves whether a system which required a patient or his appointees to make a clear advance declaration could possibly be more open to abuse than the present furtive improvisations.

One important professional reason for the doctors to take a lead in encouraging discussion is that most 'western' countries now have active societies for the legislation of voluntary euthanasia (some indeed have more than one) with a sizeable medical membership. One country, Holland, has recently legalised it.

The fact that the chaplain at one of the Dutch hospitals provides pastoral and spiritual comfort for patients who have chosen euthanasia shows, as do recent British opinion polls, that there is no uniformity of views even among the small minority of citizens who hold strong religious opinions.

The BMA generally adopts a pluralist approach in ethical matters, eventually recognising that opposing views are strongly and sincerely held and that, save in extreme emergencies, nobody should be forced to do something repugnant to their conscience.

That was the compromise reached in the case of abortion and I imagine something similar must have happened in the case of contraception—a topic which in the 1920s aroused furious controversy within our profession.

'Interfering with nature' has brought about enormous

improvements in the comfort and quality of our arrival into this world. It is about time that we devoted at least an equal amount of attention, both philosophical and technical, to the comfort and quality of our departure from it.

COLIN BREWER

VOLUNTARY EUTHANASIA AND THE DOCTORS

In 1987 the British Medical Association set up a Working Party to consider the attitude of the profession towards euthanasia in the light of the law, religious guidance, the theoretical position as then stated in the BMA *Handbook on Medical Ethics*, practice and trends existing in other countries, codes developed by other national and international medical associations and trends in public opinion. The Working Party report was published in 1988 and included the following statements in its conclusions:

Some patients see death as the fitting conclusion to the events of their life. These people may wish neither to hasten their death nor to delay it. There are limits to medical science and it is inappropriate for doctors to insist on intruding in these circumstances.

There is a distinction between an active intervention by a doctor to terminate life and a decision not to prolong life (a non-treatment decision). In both of these categories there are occasions on which a patient will ask for one of these courses of action to be taken and times when the patient could say but does not. There are also occasions when the patient is incompetent to decide.

An active intervention by anybody to terminate another person's life should remain illegal.

There are many cases where it is right that a doctor should accede to a request not to prolong the life of a patient. Appropriate medical skills and techniques should be offered when there is a good chance of providing an extension of life that will have the quality that the patient seeks.

There are many cases where it is right that a doctor should accede to a request not to prolong the life of a patient.

Appropriate medical skills and techniques should be offered when there is a good chance of providing an extension of life that will have the quality that the patient seeks.

Doctors should regard patients as authorising treatment, and should respect those authorisations and any decision to withdraw consent. But patients do not have the right to demand treatment which the doctor cannot, in conscience, provide.

Requests from young and severely disabled patients for a doctor's intervention to end their life present one of the hardest problems in day to day care. Counselling is essential to reaffirm the value of the person, and to counter pressure which may be created by the feeling of being unloved and an embarrassment to those upon whom the patient is wholly dependent.

An overwhelming majority of those who are rescued from serious suicide attempts do not repeat their attempts. This means that individuals who make such a choice about their own deaths do not always affirm this in the light of reflection.

Advance declarations are not yet recognised as binding in English or, we believe, Scottish law. They may be a valuable guide to the wishes of a patient who can no longer participate in clinical decisions, but should not be regarded as immutable or legally binding prescriptions for medical care. They require respectful attention and sensitive interpretation.

The law's deep seated adherence to intent rather than consequence alone is an important reference point in the moral assessment of any action. A decision to withdraw treatment which has become a burden and is no longer of continuing benefit to a patient, has a different intent to one which involves ending the life of a person. We accept drug treatment which may involve a risk to the patient's life if the sole intention is to relieve illness, pain, distress or suffering.

Any doctor, compelled by conscience to intervene to end a person's life, will do so prepared to face the closest scrutiny of this action that the law might wish to make.

These statements represent the most up-to-date opinions available from the BMA at the time of publication. A new BMA handbook of ethics, with a new title, is due for publication in 1993, and a further statement on the Advance Directive appears on p. 125.

When the Report was published, it provoked the following comment from the Chairman of the Voluntary Euthanasia Society, which appeared in the *British Medical Journal*:

Most people would like to have the choice of medical help to die if they judged that their quality of life was intolerable because of incurable illness. They say so in general conversation, and they have said so in professionally conducted opinion polls over many years in several countries. The BMA working party report denigrates this evidence of popular feeling. The report states: 'The Voluntary Euthanasia Society has attempted to strengthen the case for active termination of life by conducting public opinion polls which purport to show widespread agreement with the idea of active voluntary euthanasia.' The working party was given a copy of the latest such poll, carried out by National Opinion Poll in 1985. It knew that the Voluntary Euthanasia Society had not conducted the poll, and the word 'purport' implies that the results had been manipulated.

The report states that the polls discuss allowing doctors to help an incurably ill patient to an 'immediate' peaceful death and 'The sole difference between the position taken in this report and that polled is in that word'. This must surely mean that the working party approves of doctors helping patients to die, provided that they die slowly. Such help might include not using life support machines, not prescribing antibiotics or using massive doses of painkillers provided that the motive is to relieve pain and not to hasten death. This has always been called 'passive euthanasia', but we are now told that this term is wrong; it is merely good and appropriate medical care. Whatever we call it, it is welcome and a step forward from the previous stance that doctors had a duty to preserve life at all costs and under all circumstances. It may, however, still involve a long and unwelcome wait for the untreated disease to cause death.

The discussions with the patient or his representatives must, of course, occupy some time. Active voluntary euthanasia in The Netherlands involves full consultation with the patient, a second doctor; the nursing team, and, if the patient wants it, a priest. We would like to see this system adopted in Britain. An immediate death does not mean a hasty decision; it means that once the decision has been made the patient can choose the time and then die in peace.

The working party visited The Netherlands and describes the way active voluntary euthanasia is practised there. Unfortunately it does not say why it thinks the system should not work equally well in this country. The report reads as though the working party was finding arguments to support the feeling that active voluntary euthanasia is 'intuitively wrong'. Many British doctors do not feel that it is wrong, although like their Dutch counterparts they do not undertake it lightly. In spite of their strong preference for curing patients they recognise that a time may come in which acting in the patient's best interest includes responding to the wish for help to die.

A national opinion poll in 1987 found that 30 per cent of general practitioners thought that active voluntary euthanasia should be legalised and a further 15 per cent would be willing to practise it if it were legal. This body of medical opinion was not represented on the working party. Perhaps if it had been we would have been spared the repeated assertion that it is a feeling of worthlessness that leads to a request for euthanasia, and that once this mistaken feeling has been corrected the desire for euthanasia will disappear. There are many reasons for asking for euthanasia and a feeling of futility and waste may or may not play a part. One sentence in the report defies comment for its callousness: 'The few cases in which all attempts fail to alleviate distress do not appear sufficient to justify a change in the law.' How many cases would justify a change? For most of us one would be enough.

There was further comment from Dr Colin Brewer in 1990, when he reported newer, more positive developments in the field of medical ethics:

The BMA report drew what many philosophers regard as the illogical distinction between deliberately withholding life-saving treatment in the hope that the patient will die, and making sure the patient actually dies. It also suggested that active euthanasia was unacceptable to the profession. (The BMA's stance on contraception and abortion was once equally unrepresentative.)

As originally drafted, the BMA report had some contact with reality. For example, it stated: 'Any doctor compelled by conscience to intervene to end a person's life will do so prepared to face the closest scrutiny of this action that the law might wish to make.' Perhaps aware that more than 70 per cent of potential jurors favour legalising VE, it sensibly added that such a doctor 'might very well find that the court took the same view of their actions as the general public.' However, this important qualifying phrase was subsequently deleted, along with several others.

Around that time, the Institute of Medical Ethics set up a working party of its own on 'the ethics of prolonging life and assisting death'. It is chaired by Mr Geoffrey Drain, a retired trade union leader, and the secretary is the Reverend Kenneth Boyd, a Scottish theologian. To make sure that a wide range of views was available, they invited me, as a member of the VES, and Dr Gillian Ford, who represents the hospice movement. The other medical members include eminent physicians and surgeons from a wide range of disciplines, as well as nurses, philosophers, an appeal court judge and a Jesuit. Hardly a bunch of dangerous revolutionaries.

Its first report has recently been published in *The Lancet* and one conclusion in particular shows just how wrong the BMA was in claiming to speak for the profession.

On active intervention, 'the majority view' may be formulated as follows: 'A doctor acting in good conscience is ethically justified in assisting death if the need to relieve intense and increasing pain or distress caused by an incurable illness greatly outweighs the benefit to the patient of further prolonging his life. This conclusion applies to patients whose sustained wishes on this matter are known to the doctor and should thus be respected as outweighing any contrary opinion expressed by others.'

Note that the report talks of 'pain or distress'. Paralysis, breathlessness and loss of dignity or independence may not be physically painful, but they are what many people worry about most when they contemplate the end of life. They also worry about the distress their final decline may cause to their loved ones. Hospices and palliative nursing are appropriate for people who want to die in a hospice, but not everyone does and it is wrong for hospices to imply—as they are inclined to do—that they have a monopoly on virtue.

Equivalents of the VES now exist in many countries and doctors are often prominent in the membership. Voluntary euthanasia has been effectively decriminalised in Holland. A Dutch GP recently pointed out that Amsterdam is no further from London than Plymouth is and Dutch doctors are not very different from our own. Many people prefer to die at home among friends and I predict a revival of the classic deathbed farewell. GPs will therefore play an even more important part in the management of death as they do in Holland. When Britain follows Holland's lead, as it will, surveys show that many British GPs will be ready to help patients die with the dignity which is too often lacking at present.

THE FEAR OF SENILITY

Writing in the *Journal of Medical Ethics* in 1982 and 1983, Dr George Robertson, Consultant Anaesthetist at the Aberdeen Royal Infirmary, drew attention to the widespread and well-justified fear of being overtaken by senile dementia, and emphasised the need for doctors to know in advance how their patients would wish to be treated if such a fate befell them. Since then his proposals have aroused wide interest both in the medical profession and in the press. His views are set out below:

It is a curious fact that in the promotion of ideas such as mine, relating to written expression of wish, the level of public and medical interest fluctuates wildly, often for no obvious reason. Thus, long after the initial media interest in my paper in the *Journal of Medical Ethics* (Dealing with the Brain-damaged Old—Dignity before Sanctity, December 1982) there was a secondary wave of press interest which resulted in my receiving over 300 letters requesting copies of the 'Dignity Document'. These were mainly from elderly people who frequently expressed a genuine fear of senility and a strong wish to have this fear recognised by the medical profession. They clearly wanted to have some say in their medical management in senility, and recognised that by the time they were overtaken by senile dementia or major stroke the chance to have a say would have been missed.

The individual's right to accept or reject treatment, to influence his or her medical management, and to agree to organ donation when appropriate, are now part and parcel of everyday medical life. However, it is clear that in Britain, doctors seem to be resisting these changes more than their American counterparts. The individual's rights were clearly spelt out in the Report of the President's Commission on Ethical Problems in Medicine, and the use of the Living Will is now legally and medically accepted and even encouraged in several of the American States. The 'Declaration of Venice', made at the Meeting of the World Medical Association in October 1983, states that 'The physician may relieve suffering of a terminally ill patient by withholding treatment with the consent of the patient or his immediate family if unable to express his will', and 'The physician may refrain from employing any extraordinary means which would prove of no benefit for the patient'.

There are moves then, albeit rather tentative and vague, to recognise the need to listen to a patient's wishes. This is particularly clear in the care of patients with terminal cancer, and the quality of care offered by the Hospice Care Movement seems to reflect this. The profession appears to be much more insecure in preparing guidelines for dealing with the senile elderly who now constitute, numerically, a rapidly growing ethical problem. It is also this category of patients for whom the use of 'self-deliverance' is quite inappropriate because it presumably requires a minimum degree of mental and physical ability. Moreover during the past year I have detected even greater opposition within the medical profession to the concept of suicide as an acceptable means of dealing with advanced illness. Indeed I continue to receive a few letters from those who are worried and disillusioned at the prospect of taking their own lives. My personal view on this is unchanged: access to explicit information on methods of suicide is potentially dangerous and the desire to have the right to terminate life at the time when the individual chooses, although understandable in some circumstances, is fundamentally wrong and inappropriate in the management of terminal illness.

Armed with a sharper insight into dealing with the huge social problems of senility and how to define the roles of all parties involved, I accepted an invitation from the Chairman of the Central Ethical Committee of the BMA to meet the Committee in February 1984. To my knowledge the committee had discussed my proposals, along with the American Living Will, on at least three separate occasions. The Chairman has stated in the press that he found my arguments 'impressive and persuasive', and the debate was extended by a paper which I wrote to the *British Medical Journal* entitled 'Ethical Dilemmas of Brain Failure in the Elderly', which was published in December 1983. This was generally well received although a few letters in the correspondence columns of the Journal accused me of exaggerating the problem and of advocating active euthanasia.

The February meeting of the Ethical Committee was a major disappointment, particularly because the Committee was not receptive to new arguments which I put forward on patients' rights and developments in the USA. Also I argued that the medical response to the dilemmas of Intensive Care Medicine, which ultimately had to be resolved by the definition of 'brain death', was an entirely reasonable precedent for defining the limits of medical efforts to sustain life in patients with senile illness—but to no avail. In retrospect one is not entirely surprised by the Ethical Committee's stance, which expresses fear of possible legal entanglements and questions the ability of doctors to interpret prior written statements at the time of a senile illness at a particular point in the clinical course. There is also concern that an elderly person might be easily coerced by a relative into signing a document unwillingly.

It is argued that the BMA *Handbook of Medical Ethics* already gives doctors adequate guidance. In fact the book says little that could be applied directly to senility. It affirms that 'The duty of a doctor to ensure that a patient dies with dignity and as little suffering as possible remains unchanged', and recognises that the debate on the American tendency to use 'will to life' declarations 'will clearly continue for some time'. The Handbook continues: 'The doctor's basic duty is to preserve life and there is no rigid code by which such considerations as "quality of life" can be considered when deciding appropriate treatment.' It is difficult to reconcile that statement with an earlier paragraph in the book, on the question of severely malformed infants, which says, 'The doctor must attend primarily to the needs and rights of the individual infant, but in this situation he must have concern for the family as a whole. The doctor must find a just and humane solution for the infant and the family . . . ' It seems to me that there are very pertinent analogies to be drawn between the medical attitudes to patients with advanced senility. In other words, the medical guidelines seem to be prepared to acknowledge that some evaluation of 'quality of life' is admissible in the dilemmas of dealing with babies but not in the vastly more numerous dilemmas of senility.

It is with regret that I have to accuse my colleagues on the Ethical Committee of a paternalism which proclaims that the problems of senility are fundamentally medical, that the decisions are medical and that the patient's prior written opinion is not relevant.

There is evidence that those documents which have already been issued have been received quite sympathetically by general practitioners when the form is discussed and signed. It remains to be seen if sufficient mobilisation of public opinion, which seems to be very largely in favour of written wishes, can be obtained to persuade the BMA to keep the door open for further debate. I am hopeful that the evident moderate and sensible nature of my proposals will eventually win the day, but it may take some years to achieve progress. In the meantime I would hope to continue to issue a copy of the document to those who think it correctly represents their wishes on the limits to which doctors should try to maintain life in the late and often undignified stages of natural brain degeneration.

GEORGE S. ROBERTSON

MOMENT OF DEATH

I watch a clear horizon
as day ends and before night has yet begun
when the hesitant sun kisses the sea
falling lingering as on a lover's breast

And in the west I see again the dying eyes
of one whose pulse in fingering, surprised,
I had felt ebb in a minute's repartee

For in laughing he parted as in laughing zest
he lived; marvellous to rest thus in a light jest

Marvellous to fall into an ocean depth and baulk
death of its clouds

There was no difference after
except sea-birds calling loud before
had flown away in innocence.

DR S. L. HENDERSON-SMITH

DOCTORS WHO FLOUT THE LAW

The case of Dr Carr
In August 1985, Ronald Mawson, aged 63, was dying of lung cancer. The disease had spread to the spine and brain and he had developed pneumonia. Pain was kept at bay by a 'cocktail' of drugs every four hours, but he was breathless, sleepless, restless and in great distress. The doctors differed as to whether he could live for three or four days or, at the most, for three or four weeks.

Dr John Douglas Carr, who had been Mr Mawson's friend and doctor for many years, was accused at his trial in Leeds of attempting to murder his patient because, in the doctor's own words, he 'wished him to be allowed to die with dignity.' No other motive was suggested. The charge was '*attempted murder*', because death was in any case so near that the pathologist could not be sure that it had not resulted from the disease from which Mr Mawson was suffering rather than from the injection of phenobarbitone he had been given.

So far as we know, this was the first time in this country that a charge was laid against a doctor in circumstances of this kind.

Dr Carr, aged 59, was described in court as a well-loved family doctor, practising on his own with a workload of 3,500 patients. His children having grown up, he lived alone, working a 15-hour day with, as he said, 'a free afternoon on Saturday to do his shopping'. When he first came to the practice he had to overcome the handicap of a very bad stammer. This still broke through occasionally when he was being questioned in the witness box, but for the most part was kept under control by an appliance known as an 'Edinburgh masker' which, his Counsel explained, prevented the stammerer from hearing his own voice. In the dock he listened intently, but his manner was relaxed and casual.

Witnesses testified to the confidence felt for him in the neighbourhood and its dependence upon him. When they heard he was to go on trial patients and neighbours had collected 3,000 signatures to a petition in his support. In the words of a Methodist minister whose visits had often co-incided with his own, 'He really enjoys being a community doctor.'

Evidence was given of Dr Carr's special interest in the problem of the dying, in which his views were not always the same as those of the local hospice. The vice-chairman of the area Family Practitioner Committee said Dr Carr had 'a special relationship with his patients, especially with the dying, who need his attention at any time.' During his own evidence Dr Carr said reflectively, 'People find it very hard to accept the fact of death.'

In the final speech for the prosecution, Mr Rivlin urged the jury not to acquit 'a doctor minded to do this sort of thing because he has a bee in his bonnet.'

Mr Justice Mars Jones, in a summing up clearly hostile to

the defence, said that euthanasia was against the law, whether with or without the patient's consent. 'However gravely ill a man may be, however near his death, he is entitled in our laws to every hour, nay every minute of life that God has granted him. A doctor is not entitled to play God and cut short life because he believes the time has come to end the pain and suffering and to enable his patient to "die with dignity".'

The jury twice returned to the court unable to reach a verdict. After a night in a hotel, they came back to a court house which, exceptionally, had been opened on Saturday. There was a gasp of relief, and some quickly stifled applause, at the verdict of Not Guilty. The Judge refused costs to the defence, adding, 'I say no more.' And the doctor returned to his patients.

The death of King George V

Oddly, the trial of Dr Carr coincided with an article by King George V's biographer, Francis Watson (in *History Today*, December 1986), which included details of the 'euthanasia death' of the King in 1936. The account, which is based on the notebooks of the King's personal physician, Lord Dawson of Penn, reads:

From 10 o'clock onwards sleep passed gradually into stupor and coma, though the latter was never deep.' The Prince of Wales had earlier told Lord Dawson that he and the Queen had no wish for the King's life to be prolonged if the illness were judged to be mortal; but that, having made their view known, they left the decision in the doctor's hands. Dawson was in complete sympathy, and promised to direct the treatment accordingly.

The account continues with this quotation from Lord Dawson's private Sandringham notebook:

At about 11 o'clock it was evident that the last stage might endure for many hours, unknown to the Patient but little comporting with that dignity and serenity which he so richly merited and which demanded a brief final scene. Hours of waiting just for the mechanical end when all that is really life has departed only exhausts the onlookers and keeps them so strained that they cannot avail themselves of the solace of thought, communion or prayer. I therefore decided to determine the end and injected (myself) morphia gr. ¾ and shortly afterwards cocaine gr. 1 into the distended jugular vein. In about ¼ of an hour—breathing quieter—appearance more placid—physical struggle gone. Intervals between respiration lengthened, and life passed so quietly and gently that it was difficult to determine the actual moment.

The news was broadcast by the BBC at 12.10. Dawson said that one of his considerations had been 'the importance of the death receiving its first announcement in the morning papers rather than the less appropriate evening journals', and he had telephoned his wife in London to advise *The Times* to hold back publication until the announcement was made. This and his other objectives, as distinct from concern over painful and incurable disease, had been 'a different or small aspect of so-called euthanasia on which almost silently agreement now exists.'

The papers seized on these passages—a small part of Mr Watson's ten-page article—and few people can now be unaware that the King's death 'involved euthanasia'.

Most of the Press accepted the 50-year-old sensation sympathetically and lightly. Several papers contrasted the King's peaceful death with the horrifyingly prolonged end of General Franco. *The Independent* asked, 'Will this new evidence of euthanasia in high places make a difference to the chances of the law being tidied up?' and drew attention to the Advance Declaration, commenting, 'The declaration is in triplicate: the magic official number three. But not so magic as Lord Dawson's shot of morphia.' The *Daily Telegraph* published a cartoon with the caption 'But surely, doctor, if it was all right for royalty it's good enough for Mother?'

There were also many jocular comments on the favouritism shown to *The Times*. And *The Times* itself, perhaps piqued at so much tail-twisting, was one of the few to make the event the excuse for a solemn attack on voluntary euthanasia. The leader (To Hasten Death. 2 Dec. 1986), which, appropriately, took its arguments from those of half a century ago, inspired the following definitive reply:

Sir, Your leading article repeating various objections to the campaign for voluntary euthanasia, in the light of recent cases (December 2), is vitiated by four false arguments.

The practical objection that the cases of George V and Ronald Mawson are not relevant to the issue of voluntary euthanasia ignores the fact that such cases are excellent examples of what is wrong with the present system—or rather, lack of system.

The medical objection that dying patients are not in a fit condition to make rational decisions about life and death is precisely the reason why advocates of voluntary euthanasia propose a declaration made when patients are in a fit condition to make decisions about either not being given further medical treatment or being given euthanasia.

The legal objection that there would be abuses if euthanasia were legalised is precisely the reason why advocates of voluntary euthanasia propose a declaration made before a competent witness to prevent the sort of abuses which could occur—and which do occur now, when medical attendants make decisions without proper consideration or consultation, and when voluntary euthanasia is confused with involuntary euthanasia.

The moral objection that euthanasia violates the sanctity of life ignores the fact that this principle is already broken by the state in cases of war and capital punishment and by individuals in cases of suicide and self-defence (and by most human beings in cases of animals used as pets or for food). Advocates of voluntary euthanasia propose that the criterion should be the quality rather than the sanctity of life, and that the decision about the quality of life should be made by the person living it rather than by outside moral, legal, or medical experts.

But the main arguments for voluntary euthanasia, which are generally ignored by its opponents (and in your leading article), are that the right to life includes the right to leave life, which includes the right to be helped on the way with proper safeguards, and that the great majority of the population favours the legalisation of this right.

NICOLAS WALTER
Rationalist Press Association

The slippery slope of euthanasia

Fifty years ago, we are now told, the dying George V was helped out of life with a large injection. The same thing happened more recently, perhaps by chance, to a dying lung cancer patient, Ronald Mawson: the doctor was a local GP, Dr John Carr. The chief difference is that Carr was prosecuted for attempted murder in Leeds Crown Court.

In spite of an adverse summing up by the judge, the jury acquitted him. Perhaps they had a collective disinclination to convict a doctor whom they believed to have acted honourably and mercifully. Today there is a widespread feeling, which the dubious blessings of high-tech medicine have increased, that, in the words of another court case survivor, Dr John Bodkin Adams, 'Easing the passing of a dying person isn't all that wicked. She wanted to die—that can't be murder.'

We do not know if Mr Mawson wanted to die; we do not know what may have passed between him and his doctor, and many would regard this as an important missing element in the case. However if Mr Mawson, fatally ill and in pain, did want to die, that would make no difference in law.

Although suicide has not been a crime since 1961, the change did not confer any positive right on an individual to dispose of his own life—an odd hangover of ecclesiastical law into a secular age. Nor can anyone else legally help you: assisting suicide remains a crime—and when the assistance is particularly active any resulting charge is likely to be not just 'assisting a suicide' but 'attempted murder', as in the prosecution of Charlotte Hough in 1983.

Yet the word 'murder' brings in whole trains of irrelevant associations with sawn-off shotguns or bodies buried on the moors, and in practice most people *do* make a strong moral distinction between murder and what is increasingly known as 'mercy killing'.

This headline-term is in itself an unsatisfactory one. Its implication is that the sufferer in need of mercy plays a passive role in the whole affair while one of Nature's grown-ups, doctor or other, comes in to play Angel of Death. There, indeed, are innumerable occasions on which this has happened, and only rarely, through ill luck or mismanagement, does the matter end up in court. But it cannot be emphasised too strongly that the euthanasia issue is not essentially about the terminally ill being helped through their final stage but about people having the right to take their *own* decision.

This is just another aspect of the debate about individual autonomy over our own lives which has been in process in all developed societies for at least two generations. Inch by inch, we have argued our democratic way through divorce, contraception, abortion, parents' rights, children's rights and the last bastion is, appropriately, death.

In no other sphere of our lives does the State still withhold decision-making from us. Is it surprising that, accustomed as we are today to autonomy and choice at other crucial moments, we are becoming rebellious about being told that we have no choice about our dying?

My own experience is that doctors today are much less inclined to know best for their patients than they were even ten years ago. But, for this very reason, patient demand for the Final Say is likely to become more open. It looks as if, whether we like it or not (and some don't like it at all), the idea of having a say in one's own dying is going to become a reality.

Whatever one's view, it should be realised that this is a movement concerned with quality of life *not* with devaluing life. It is not a sinister conspiracy to destroy the weak but an attempt to allow people to go on being themselves till the end. The difficulties of framing a new law that would not be subject to abuse are great, but let us at least try before we take refuge in that bleat about it being 'the slippery slope to the gas ovens'.

This idea is based on the mistaken impression that the Nazis 'started with' euthanasia and then progressed morally downwards. Nazi doctrine negated individual choice from the start, had nothing to do with 'happy dying' and merely hijacked the old, benign term 'euthanasia' as a cover.

It is understandable that as soon as anyone mentions gas

ovens all rational discussion becomes side-tracked, but this is really not an adequate response to a complex and increasingly pressing debate. Yes, there is a slippery slope here—but it is, rather, the evasive slide into empty moralising resorted to by those who are afraid to recognise an issue whose time has come.

GILLIAN TINDALL

EUTHANASIA AND THE NURSES

Euthanasia—passive and active, voluntary and involuntary—is being discussed more and more by nurses, especially those working in geriatric wards, as well as by the nursing press.

The following is a selection of recent views.

Last rights

This year, between 5,000 and 6,000 Dutch people will be given, quite legally, a gentle and easy death—that is, euthanasia. The decision must be 'undertaken by a medical practitioner who may not delegate this task to a third party', for example, a member of the family or nursing staff.

The Dutch nurses in a recently reported case broke the law by ending their patient's life on their own decision, not on medical instructions. In England they would face criminal charges, whether acting on their own behalf or on a doctor's orders. The Royal College of Nursing's view, in line with this law, is that 'the practice of euthanasia is contrary to the public interest and to medical and nursing ethical principles as well as to natural and civil rights and (the college) is opposed to the introduction of any legislation permitting euthanasia.'

But despite the RCN's unequivocal rejection, it would seem that euthanasia is not confined to Holland, or to Dutch nurses. My experience suggests that British nurses are often involved in euthanasia, if by euthanasia we mean 'a deliberately life-shortening act or the deliberate omission of a life-lengthening act in respect of an incurable patient, in such patients' interests'. This covers both passive euthanasia, that is omission, and active euthanasia, a life-shortening act.

There have been rare situations in England where nurses have acted on their own initiative and, for example, turned down a patient's ventilator. But the more usual cases are ones in which the nurse acts on the doctor's instructions or observes and condones his action. The difficulty in assessing the extent of these practices is obvious, given their illegality on the one hand, and the pressure not to 'tell on colleagues' on the other. One nurse I spoke to, for instance, told me how a doctor prescribed morphine for a recently hospitalised elderly stroke victim. The nurse thought the medication was both unnecessary and dangerous. The pharmacy confirmed her view. The nurse manager, who was told the story, counselled the nurse in such a way as to suggest that she—and not the doctor—stood to risk disciplinary proceedings. In the event the drug was given by another nurse and within hours the woman died.

A more common scenario is where the nurse is involved and supports the doctor's intentions. For instance, one district nurse arrived at a patient's home to find the doctor there. The patient was terminally ill, restless and apparently in distress. His wife was exhausted. The nurse gave the morphine prescribed and left on the unspoken understanding that the doctor would also give some medication to end the patient's life. When she returned a couple of hours later, the patient was dead. She felt grateful, she told me, for the doctor's courage and kindness.

In this case, the doctor or nurse—as it is often the case that she gives the drug—may well have argued that the extra dose of morphine was given with the primary intention of easing the patient's suffering, although the consequence might well be to shorten life.

This would not necessarily protect one from the charge of murder. Yet anecdotal evidence from nurses' involvement in euthanasia would seem to put it almost in the category of 'custom and practice'.

There is some evidence that British courts are inclined to leniency, as in the case of Dr John Carr, who was acquitted of murder despite admitting he injected phenobarbitone into a terminally ill patient to 'allow him to die with dignity'.

The Houghtons, who killed their paralysed son, Robert, were also acquitted. Following the judgement, Janet Houghton told Dr Christiaan Barnard, 'Of course I hated giving him those pills, but who else would have done it?' It is perhaps ironic that Dr Barnard, noted for his high technology life-saving operations, is strongly in favour of euthanasia and says that 'at times a doctor may have to decide, however reluctantly, that death is the best option'. He believes the physician, not Mrs Houghton, should have made that decision and given the pills.

The truth is that professionals are uncomfortable with this position. It is acceptable, it would seem, to practise passive euthanasia. But active euthanasia is still generally decried by doctors and nurses. It is acceptable to turn off ventilators, to withhold antibiotics or adequate nutrition and to decide 'not for resuscitation', 'nursing care only', but not actively to provide an 'easy and gentle death'. Dr Barnard feels that we are dodging our responsibilities by preferring 'not even to think about it'.

In Holland the decision to provide euthanasia is theoretically always reached by consensus. A team of doctors, nurses and clergy and, where possible, the patient and relatives are party to the discussion.

It is an interesting solution to one aspect of the problem and one that should surely be openly debated within the nursing profession since the present situation, as much as any other, may be open to abuse. Nurses often suffer great stress in the long time before death occurs through non-intervention which they may feel adds unnecessary suffering to the family, and possibly the patient. It can also be argued that the decision to seek aid-in-dying is as much a patient's right as any other part of their care—for instance, refusing antibiotics.

There are no easy solutions, but the RCN's total rejection of euthanasia in all its complex aspects is surely no longer tenable for the nurse in the clinical setting. A recent article maintained that it is not only desirable, but vital that the nursing profession take part in an open debate on the subject. The article ended with the question: 'Has nursing risen to this challenge?' So far the answer seems to be, no.

PAT TURTON

From a letter received by the Voluntary Euthanasia Society
It is customary for the relatives of a sick geriatric patient to be asked if they wish for a chest infection, for example, to be treated with antibiotics. About half do not. Many of the patients themselves refuse to eat and drink, and will actively spit out food and liquids. They can get very hostile to the carer, and if a naso-gastric tube is put down to feed them 50 per cent will pull it up. This may be either because they are confused or perhaps because they consciously want to die.

I have known a patient to survive on water for five weeks, emaciated but still determinedly refusing sustenance. Then doctors move in, probably because the situation is too harrowing for the relatives and staff. It is decided that the patient is in pain, even though there may be no sign of this. He is then put on to Mist Bromptons, a drug concoction for terminal patients which contains diamorphine or cocaine and a tranquilliser, and this will sooner or later release him from his bondage to life.

On the wards I have been on for the past ten years none of the nursing staff has ever objected, for we see the poor quality of some of the patients' lives and realise that they may have determined to commit suicide in the only way they can. But some time a do-gooder is going to object, and then there could be an outcry. At present the patients, by whatever means, do often achieve their ends, but I wish with all my heart that we could be allowed to put them out of their misery by an injection. What would happen if one kept an animal alive under these conditions?

Recently I nursed a Belsen-thin geriatric of 80. For a period of two years she had all the nursing care we could give, including antibiotic treatment. This was because her son would not let her die with dignity even though she had a chest infection. No one should have the power to make another 'live' when they are 50 per cent dead—but they do. What would *your* relatives say?

AN SRN

The quality of dying
For some time I have had both a need to shout: 'I wish some of my patients were dead,' and a certainty that many who heard me would not believe in my affection and care for them.

Let us look at the 26 women on this ward. Nine are not demented; they have been in hospitals for decades, and I exclude them. The other 17 have all come to hospital comparatively recently. They have nearly all lived full normal lives in the outside world for more than 70 or 80 years until their dementia brought them here. They may have arrived a few months ago. Some have lived here for as many as ten years.

Three of the 17 demented patients seem content. Mary, Gertie and Faith all laugh with us a lot and make easy contact. Though none of these three holds a rational conversation for even a few sentences, they are well satisfied with the 'good chats' we have together.

Joyce is not always content, but I believe she accepts her condition. I was astounded when I heard the following conversation. Ruth, a new patient, rounded on Joyce: 'You really are such a silly!' she said. 'Ruth, that's unkind!' I said. Joyce was laughing. 'Oh I don't mind,' she responded. 'I thought it was rather . . . (searching for the right word) . . . appropriate.'

Nancy has presenile dementia and has apparently passed beyond having any emotional involvement in her life. But what of Ann, Olive and Paula? I am now thinking of some of the 12 residents whose feelings are often distressed.

How Ann's moods swing! We come on duty and her face lights up. She advances on us, arms outstretched to hug us; she hugs us on and off throughout a shift. In blacker moods she glares, she draws away and she shouts. But if we stay with her through such a mood she will break down and sob. 'I know,' I tell her then. 'It's rotten here, isn't it?' A tiny nod. 'Cry as much as you want to, Ann, I would too, if I lived here. It's all right for me. I can go home when my work is finished, can't I?' We give each other a special hug, hard.

But her friend Olive—they walk up and down together all

day—cannot be reached in her patches of distress. 'Mummy, mummy, mummy,' she whimpers, as we try to sit her on the lavatory or wash her face. 'I want my mummy!'

I grieve for them at these times. I know why nurses have sometimes been taught that it is unwise to become emotionally involved with patients. However, even the detached nurse must have feelings of her own. As I have when I am trying to help Paula, who hangs on to her pants and pulls them up as I try to pull them down. She hangs on to me and hinders me as I try to pull her pants back up. She tears off the serviettes that are essential to protect her clothes at mealtimes.

'Paula! I am trying to help you,' I cry. And just occasionally, when it has been an exceptionally trying morning, I scream inside myself: 'Oh, what is the point of it all? If only these patients could see that we are trying to help them. If only outsiders could see this. If only those who are so sure that life is worthwhile to the very end could come and do this work for a month or two!'

Paula, too, can catch our eyes and laugh and look happy sometimes. At other times she looks at us with a long, lost and wondering look. 'Who are you?' that look asks.

There are the patients' feelings, the nurses' feelings and the relatives' feelings. A relative often needs our help more than the patient herself. A daughter, an only child, was letting herself go the other day: 'You nurses know what dementia is like, of course. For lots of us it is only a word. We know nothing about it until it hits our family. I had no idea it was like this.'

That daughter dares to recognise her mother's condition, how she feels about it, and that she needs to, and can, scream out loud. Many relatives cannot accept that 'it is like this'. They need much comfort and support, but they do not allow us to be wholly honest with them.

I believe that the time will come—and I think it should—when we may choose, *only if we wish*, while of sound mind and after careful consideration, to bow out of life at some future date, if life ever becomes intolerable and without reasonable prospect of recovery. The time will vary with the individual. Some will choose the time themselves; some will trust a loving relative, or even caring hospital staff, to choose it for them.

I have thought about this for some time. I have listened to and considered all the arguments against voluntary euthanasia. And, despite my fear that if I spoke out even my colleagues would not understand, I have now discussed this with others. Many have been grateful to be given the opportunity to share their similar feelings with me. I am far from being the only nurse for whom the prospect of going on and on as wretchedly as some of our patients, is too awful to contemplate.

MARGARET ARRAL

Final comment
When a patient in hospital suffers a heart attack, the emergency 'crash' team is called to carry out resuscitation. *But*, in the medical notes of some patients can be found a 'Do Not Resuscitate' (DNR) order. Nurses follow this by not calling the crash team if the patient has a cardiac arrest.

DNR orders are used when cardiopulmonary resuscitation is thought to be futile, or inappropriate due to poor quality of life; but a recent survey of DNR orders in a Liverpool district general hospital showed that there are no clear local guidelines for their use, and that there is extremely poor communication of orders between doctors and nurses. As a result, some patients were receiving quite inappropriate resuscitation, whereas the crash team was not called for some patients although they had become suitable for resuscitation.

The survey showed that relatives were rarely consulted, and there was no mention of patients currently being involved in the decision-making.

The survey's results are probably typical of the situation in all UK hospitals. It paints a worrying picture of confusion and lack of consultation with patients over crucial medical decisions. The report calls for local guidelines on when crash calls become inappropriate, more reviews of individual patients, and far more discussion between all members of the medical team, the patient, and relatives. These suggestions should be adopted urgently in all hospitals.

The Law and the Pressure Groups

Through endless days of struggling breath
He watched the world grow small and far:
He met the steadfast eyes of death,
And haply saw how kind they are.

JOHN BUCHAN
on the death of his brother

Since the Suicide Act 1961 it has not been a crime in the United Kingdom to take one's own life. However, Subsection 2(1) of the Act states:

A person who aids, abets, counsels or procures the suicide of another, or an attempt by another to commit suicide shall be liable on conviction on indictment to imprisonment for a term not exceeding fourteen years.

Scottish law differs slightly from English law on this point, in that it is not a crime or an offence to *advise* a person as to how 'life', as we understand the word, may be terminated, although it is a serious offence, carrying the risk of imprisonment, to assist a person to commit suicide by administering drugs or using other physical means, and a doctor may not prescribe drugs to a patient known to be contemplating suicide.

The aim of the Voluntary Euthanasia Society and the Voluntary Euthanasia Society of Scotland is to change the law, so that someone who finds life intolerable because of an incurable condition can receive medical help to die. Safeguards would be built into the law to ensure that no other solution acceptable to that person is overlooked and that any decision is made sensitively. The following historical survey of the movement was written by Barbara Smoker.

The Voluntary Euthanasia Society

The seeds of the Voluntary Euthanasia Society (Britain) and of the subsequent worldwide movement were planted, and took root, in the 1931 presidential address of Dr C. Killick Millard, MD., DSc., to the Society of Medical Officers of Health. His speech, entitled 'A Plea for the Legalisation of Voluntary Euthanasia under Certain Conditions', was then published as a pamphlet, with an introduction by the eminent surgeon, Sir William Arbuthnot Lane, and with a draft Bill appended; and the revolutionary proposal received widespread publicity.

Four years of correspondence on the subject ensued between Dr Millard and other interested members of the medical and other professions. They met in Leicester in January 1935, and set up a small steering committee—comprising three doctors, three clergymen, and a solicitor. Within a few months, Millard had brought in more supporters, including three distinguished churchmen—Dean Inge, W. R. Matthews and Dick Sheppard; and a consultative medical committee was formed, comprising eight eminent doctors. (So far, the total financial turnover of the movement amounted to £24.12s.5d.)

In October 1935, the Voluntary Euthanasia Legalisation Society was formally founded, with Lord Moynihan as President, C. J. Bond as Chairman, Rev. A. S. Hurn as Treasurer, and Dr C. Killick Millard as Honorary Secretary. The following became Vice-Presidents: Rev. Prof. Creed, Lord and Lady Denman, Havelock Ellis, Lord Henley, Julian Huxley, Sir William Arbuthnot Lane, Harold Laski, Lord Listowel (its President today, fifty years later), Rev. H. D. A. Major, Sir Roderick Meiklejohn, Lord Ponsonby, Eleanor Rathbone, Sir Humphrey Rolleston, and Sir Arnold Wilson.

Two months later, on 10 December—now, coincidentally, Human Rights Day—the inaugural public meeting was held at BMA House, London. On 4 February, 1936, a consultative legal council was established under the chairmanship of

Professor Winfield, and in November 1936 Lord Ponsonby introduced the Voluntary Euthanasia (Legislation) Bill in the House of Lords.

Though it fell at its second reading, this Bill generated considerable public discussion, gaining for the Voluntary Euthanasia Legalisation Society new members and supporters, including, again, many who were distinguished in the arts, sciences, and professions. But it was to be another three decades (1969) before the next voluntary euthanasia Bill would be introduced—and again unsuccessfully. Meanwhile, however, the Suicide Act was passed in 1961—removing suicide from the criminal law, though making it a criminal offence to assist in the suicide of another. Most recently, a Bill in 1990 failed to gain a majority.

In 1969, the Society dropped the word 'Legalisation' from its name. Then, at the 1979 annual meeting, the name was again changed—for the sake of modernity—to Exit. Three years later, however, it was decided by a large majority of the membership (in a postal referendum) to revert to the former name, the Voluntary Euthanasia Society.

This was at least partly due to the adverse publicity the Society had sustained when, in 1981, the Society's then secretary was convicted of conspiring to assist a number of suicides. Although the VES dissociated itself from his abuse of his position in thus pre-empting euthanasia legislation, its public image was certainly tarnished by it, and the Society has found it an uphill struggle to regain its reputation as a respectable pressure-group rather than, as one newspaper, (*The Times*, October 31, 1981) dubbed it, a 'suicide club'.

In 1979 a proposal had been mooted that the VES publish a practical guide to rational suicide ('self-deliverance')—a sort of 'do-it-yourself' manual, as a stop-gap expedient, pending the legalisation of active voluntary euthanasia that would be medically induced. Legal opinions on the proposed publication were obtained, only to cancel one another out.

While the VES membership was overwhelmingly in favour of publishing the guide—and, indeed its pre-publication publicity brought a sudden surge in membership from about 2,000 to 11,000—the executive was divided. Even after the election (in October 1980) of a new executive that was largely committed to publication, this was further delayed by a member of the Society applying for a civil injunction. An amendment was then made to the Society's constitution, so as to bring a publication of this kind within its purview.

Meanwhile, the fact that the specific law against assisting the suicide of another does not apply in Scotland persuaded the newly formed Scottish Exit to bring out its own similar guide (entitled *How to Die with Dignity*), which thus, in September 1980, became the first such publication in the world. The more comprehensive English *Guide to Self-Deliverance* finally appeared in June 1981, soon to be followed by similar publications in France, Germany, Switzerland and the USA.

But the English booklet was almost immediately threatened with criminal prosecution by the Director of Public Prosecutions. This threat, however, was then modified—first to one of a civil injunction, to be sought by the Attorney-General, and then to a mere application by him to the High Court for a 'declaration' of illegality under section 2 of the Suicide Act, 1961. In the event, on 28 April, 1983, Mr Justice Woolf turned down the Attorney-General's declaration of the law, finding in favour of the VES—with costs.

The press reports, which this time were mainly friendly to the Society, again led to an increased spurt in membership applications—a spurt which had already begun as a result of the widely, and most sympathetically, reported 'self-deliverance' (on 3 March, 1983) of the world-renowned writer, Arther Koestler, incurably ill with Parkinson's disease and leukaemia. Koestler was vice-president of the VES and author of (alongside his better-known writings) the preface to the Society's *Guide to Self-Deliverance*.

However, in spite of its technical victory, the guide was not really given total clearance by Mr Justice Woolf. Although he held that publishing such factual information was not unlawful, he also said that the legality of distributing it would depend on there being no intent (either individually or in general) 'to assist those who are contemplating suicide'.

Stocks of the booklet, of which almost 9,000 copies had been sold to members, happened to run out at about this time; and the VES executive had to decide whether to reprint it as it was or take the opportunity to revise it or not to reissue it at all. Finally, on a majority vote, it was decided that the guide should not be reissued. The two main reasons for this were: first, the guide was felt, increasingly, to be of limited usefulness to those who were ill or disabled enough to need physical aid to suicide or who were unable to obtain the required drugs—its chief importance, perhaps, being seen in the context of freedom of information rather than that of functional do-it-yourself euthanasia; and secondly, the Woolf judgement appeared to prevent the Society from distributing the guide in any useful way within the law—and to keep within the law was imperative as long as the VES wished to continue, as its primary aim, to press for legislation.

A random-sample postal survey of members of Exit (as it then was) living in England and Wales was carried out in 1981 by Rosalind Lam, for the Institute for Social Studies in Medical Care—and a summary of the results, analysed with particular reference to statistical suicide 'risk', took up a full page of *The Times Health Supplement* on 30 October, 1981. It shows that two-thirds of the members replying were aged 60 and over, and only 6 per cent were under the age of 40. Women outnumbered men by three to two. Nearly half the women and more than a quarter of the men were living alone (a significantly higher proportion than for the general population of the same ages). Asked to describe their health for their age as excellent, good, fair, or poor, almost three-quarters of the respondents answered 'excellent' or 'good'. Witnessing the slow death of a relative or friend was given by one in four as their reason for joining the Society. Three-quarters came from non-manual occupations—the majority from the professions—and 7 per cent were, or had been, nurses. Only 43 per cent had a religious affiliation, though almost all had had a religious upbringing.

A public opinion survey conducted by Mass Observation throughout Britain in 1969 showed 51 per cent of the population in favour of active voluntary euthanasia; a similar poll conducted by National Opinion Polls in 1976 showed an increase in favour to 69 per cent; and a repetition of the same question, in a survey again conducted by National Opinion

Polls, for VES, in February, 1985 (as a run-up to the Society's Golden Jubilee celebrations), shows a further increase to 72 per cent in favour. The most recent survey, conducted in 1989, showed 75 per cent in favour, with 32 per cent agreeing strongly.

Similar statistical surveys are carried out every four years in the USA (conducted by Harris). These showed only 37 per cent in favour of active voluntary euthanasia in that country in 1973, but a steady increase since then, culminating in 61 per cent in favour in January 1985.

Regional analysis of the 1989 British (NOP) survey shows that the highest percentage of the population in favour of voluntary euthanasia is in the South West (81 per cent), while the lowest is in East Anglia, Wales and the North West (70 per cent). There is little statistical difference in terms of sex or economic class, but there is a certain age divergence—the younger respondents now tending to be more in favour of voluntary euthanasia than the older age groups.

All the main religious denominations (including RC) in Britain show a majority in favour of active voluntary euthanasia. Roman Catholics (self-declared) show 48 per cent, and members of the Church of England 78 per cent, in favour.

In 1991 the Society drew up an Advance Directive or Living Will by which people can make their wishes known with regard to medical treatment in cases of incurable illness or incapacity. In the opinion of learned counsel it is effective in English Law and must be followed by a doctor when treating a patient.

The subject, reports John Warden, parliamentary correspondent of the *British Medical Journal*, 'is sure to be on the legal and parliamentary agenda in the coming months. Attention will focus on a case in Winchester, where allegations of euthanasia have resulted in a senior consultant being charged with attempted murder. The prosecution, like another (which failed) in 1990, concerns the administration of potassium chloride, in this case to an elderly woman who was disabled by arthritis.

'The court proceedings will be closely watched by an all party parliamentary group of MPs and peers that was formed last year to review the case for legalising euthanasia. The new group, under the chairmanship of a medical peer, Lord Winstanley, is financed and serviced by the Voluntary Euthanasia Society. In 1992 it decided to sponsor an exploratory bill in the House of Lords to legitimise the 'living will' or Advance Directive.

'Any bill would be, more than anything, a device to raise the issue in debate. The chances of substantive legislation on any aspect of euthanasia are still considered to be remote. Although the euthanasia society claims that about 90 MPs are sympathetic to euthanasia, few openly support it, and there has never been a serious attempt in the Commons to legislate for euthanasia.

'The present drive reflects the extent to which a taboo has been lifted, but it is only the start of what promises to be a long drawn out campaign, possibly over two or more parliaments. Against it, the pro-life group of peers and MPs—best known as an anti-abortion lobby—has regrouped to make the fight against euthanasia its top priority.'

Meanwhile the groundswell of public opinion is growing. The following article was published in *The Economist* in March 1988:

Die as you choose

In one of the world's smaller countries, mercy-killing is accepted by the medical establishment and openly practised a few thousand times each year. In one of the world's biggest countries, euthanasia is condemned by the medical establishment, secretly practised many times more often, and almost never comes to light. Which of these countries has a mercy-killing doctor now languishing in its jails? It is the small one, Holland, which has rules for euthanasia and so can police it effectively. The Dutch doctor broke his country's rules. There is a moral here, and not just for the big death-forbidding country, America, which is now going over the arguments about euthanasia once again.

In January 1988 the *Journal* of the American Medical Association published a bizarre letter in which an anonymous doctor claimed to have killed a 20-year-old cancer patient at her own request. The letter was probably written for polemical impact. It is scarcely credible. Its author claims that he (or she) met the cancer patient for the first time, heard five words from her—'Let's get this over with'—then killed her. Even the most extreme proponents of euthanasia do not support such an action in those circumstances.

Yet medical monstrosities that are hardly any better undoubtedly continue, almost as a matter of macabre routine, in America, Britain and many other countries. It is disturbingly easy to find doctors who will say, in private, that they sometimes kill patients on purpose. Most say they know somebody else who does. But because they can rarely discuss euthanasia openly with patients—even when those patients beg them for it—doctors tend to kill only when the dying are too far gone to consent. Thus, because voluntary euthanasia is taboo, a doctor makes the decision himself—and the patient is killed involuntarily in the night with a syringe. That is one price of keeping euthanasia secret.

If all forms of mercy-killing are wrong, they should remain taboo. But are they? Because many people accept that it is sad, undignified and gruesome to prolong the throes of death with all the might of medical technology, passive euthanasia—letting patients die—is widely accepted. Most American states have 'living-will' legislation that protects doctors from prosecution if they do not try to save someone who has said he does not want life prolonged. Active euthanasia—killing—remains controversial. How long can the distinction between killing and letting die hold out?

Just as there can be culpable omissions, so too can there be blameless acts. Suppose—to take an example from the moral-philosophy books—that a man stands to gain from the death of a certain child. The child strikes his head in the bath and falls unconscious. The man sits down and watches him drown. The fact that the man has performed no action does not excuse him. Similarly, suppose that a doctor does no wrong by withholding some treatment in order that death should come sooner rather than later. Is he then necessarily wrong if he administers enough pain-killers to kill? Does the fact that the doctor performed an action, rather than an omission, condemn him?

Many doctors working on the battlefield of terminal suffering think that only squeamishness demands a firm difference between passive and active euthanasia on request. Their argument for killing goes like this: one of a doctor's duties is to prevent suffering; sometimes that is all there is left for him to do, and killing the only way to do it. There is nothing new in this view. When Hippocrates formulated his oath for doctors, which explicitly rules out active killing, most other Greek doctors and thinkers disagreed with his ban.

Some people believe that the time of death is appointed by God and that no man should put the clock back on another. Yet if a patient's philosophical views embrace euthanasia, it is not clear why the religious objections of others should intrude on his death. Another worry is that a legal framework for euthanasia, permitting a doctor to comply with a dying man's request in a prescribed set of circumstances might pose dangers for society by setting a precedent for killing. That depends on the society. Holland, arguably, is ready for it. It is probably no coincidence that it was Dutch doctors who most heroically resisted pressure to join in the Nazi medical atrocities that have given euthanasia its worst name. The same tenacious respect for individual liberty that stopped them killing healthy people, who did not want to die, now lets them help dying people who do.

Germany, by contrast, will not be able to legalise any form of euthanasia for a long time to come. Opposition is too fierce, because of the shadow of the past. Countries with an uninterrupted recent libertarian tradition have less to fear from setting some limited rules for voluntary euthanasia. By refusing to discuss it, they usher in something worse.

THE SITUATION WORLDWIDE

Australia
In Australia attitudes among the medical profession and the public are changing in favour of euthanasia. Euthanasia is currently illegal in all of the six states and two territories that make up the federal system of Australia.

The state of Victoria has enacted legislation—unique among the Australian states and territories—on refusal of medical treatment. This act makes it a criminal offence to treat a patient against his or her wishes. Patients can name an agent to make decisions on their treatment if they become unable to decide for themselves.

South Australia and the Northern Territories have Natural Death Acts, which are similar to 'living will' legislation in some states of the US.

In 1988 the Centre for Human Bioethics at Monash University in Melbourne surveyed 2,000 doctors in Victoria and found that 869 supported voluntary euthanasia. One third said that they had been involved in voluntary euthanasia at least once. Nearly half said that they would practise voluntary euthanasia if it was legal. Early results from a survey by the School for Community Medicine in the University of New South Wales indicate that withdrawal of treatment is a major ethical issue among practitioners.

So far intensive care specialists have been extremely cautious about discussing the issue in public. Their main line is that they will do nothing illegal. But many will withdraw life support when there is no hope of recovery and allow the dying process to occur with dignity by administering sedatives and analgesics. Active support of accelerated dying is not acknowledged.

PETER POCKLEY

Canada

It is a criminal offence to help anyone to commit suicide in Canada, but three recent widely publicised cases have raised questions about whether people should have the right to determine the time of their own deaths with medical help.

A 24-year-old woman in Quebec, known as Nancy B, has asked the Quebec Superior Court to order the hospital where she has been in intensive care for 30 months to disconnect the mechanical respirator that is keeping her alive. The court moved to her bedside to hear her testimony. Her doctor said that she would die within minutes once the respirator was disconnected. The woman, paralysed by Guillain-Barré syndrome since 1989, told the judge that she can no longer tolerate her existence. The court is expected to give its decision soon.

In British Columbia Dr Tom Perry, a pharmacologist and cabinet minister, publicly revealed that he and members of his family who are medical professionals had taken turns to give morphine to their father, who was dying of cancer. He admitted that the drug may have hastened his father's death. He said that his reason for speaking out was to open up public discussions on euthanasia.

The governing body of the medical profession has made its position clear after criticising the action of Dr Peter Graff, an internal medicine specialist, who prescribed doses of morphine that hastened the deaths of two gravely ill patients. This is the first time that a doctors' regulatory body in Canada has had to deal with euthanasia. Dr Graff argued in his own defence that he did not consider his actions to be euthanasia but simply an attempt to relieve suffering. The coroner's inquiry concluded that both patients died after morphine overdoses.

The Canadian House of Commons has a private member's bill before it that would enable doctors to comply with a dying patient's wish to die sooner without the doctor facing legal charges. A recent public opinion poll found that 75 per cent of Canadians favour mercy killings of incurably ill patients if the patient's request is in writing.

Earlier this year the Ontario Medical Association concluded that the issue of euthanasia should be left for society to determine, not the medical profession. It said that doctors should not take the lead in publicly debating the question but should, if asked, provide scientific information that might help the public to make a decision.

The Canadian Medical Association (CMA) has long stated that it is not unethical for a doctor to withhold heroic treatment that could prolong the life of a terminally ill patient. This in effect condones passive euthanasia but not active euthanasia to speed death. At its annual meeting last summer the CMA's committee on ethics reported that it had not finished revising the association's policy on euthanasia and was granted additional time to complete its report.

M. DUNLOP

France

It is quite common in France, as in many other countries, to give patients who are terminally ill a 'lytic cocktail', an overdose of a sedative or another lethal substance. But euthanasia is likely to remain in a legislative no man's land because legislation would, in the words of the neonatologist Alexandre Minkowski, 'institutionalise provoked death'.

Last year the cancer specialist Léon Schwartzenberg was temporarily suspended by the Council de l'Ordre des Médecins, France's medical association, for declaring that he had helped some of his terminally ill patients to die. A member of the European parliament and briefly France's minister of health, Dr Schwartzenberg later submitted a proposal on euthanasia to the European parliament, stating, 'When a physician decides, in all conscience, to answer the insistent and permanent request of a patient to help him stop his existence, that has lost all dignity in his eyes, he acts in respect of a human life.' He said that he wanted euthanasia to be better understood. 'There is no question of establishing a law—particularly in a country like France . . . where everything that is legal is seen as normal.'

The National Ethical Committee, presided over by the haematologist Dr Jean Bernard, also opposes the legalisation of euthanasia because it believes that a law would be abused and wrongly interpreted and would give doctors 'an exorbitant power over the life of an individual.' The committee recognised that the patient's request might be reasonable but it might be made ambivalently. What was worse, economic, family, or ideological considerations unrelated to the patient's distress, or even the shortage of hospital beds or a family's impatience to inherit, might play a part in the decision. Moreover, said Dr Bernard, 'We now have the means to fight against pain.'

Father Michel Riquet, of the Society of Jesus, has commented that the word euthanasia is ambiguous. It literally means 'good death' in Greek, and in the middle ages there were good death fraternities that aimed not at shortening patients' lives but at providing them with palliative care for their pain and moral and spiritual comfort to help them die in dignity and as Christians. Father Riquet points out that the 'interdiction to kill' pronounced by Pope Pius XII did not imply the obligation to use all possible and extraordinary means to prolong a life that was moving towards its end.

ALEXANDER DOROZYNSKI

Germany

In German law the penal codes for first and second degree murder state fairly clearly that active euthanasia is a crime against human life and punishable by up to five years in prison. Even during the Third Reich, when active euthanasia was practised on a wide scale on mentally ill patients, it was never formally legalised.

Passive euthanasia, the denial of life prolonging treatment to a terminally ill patient, has always been regarded in law as a matter between doctors and their patients. The doctor is left to decide when life prolonging measures have become futile; the patient or, if he or she is incapable of making such a decision, the relatives then decide whether or not such measures should be continued. There is no known case of a German court questioning a patient's right to reject clearly inadequate and inefficient treatment.

Suicide and assisting a suicidal action are not forbidden by German law. Penal Code article 216 forbids only 'killing on request', which carries the threat of between six months' and five years' imprisonment. This caused a great stir in 1984 when Dr Julius Hackethal of Erlangen, a professor of surgery and a popular author, publicly admitted that he had helped a patient with cancer to commit suicide by providing a toxic agent. But Dr Hackethal escaped prosecution, as did Dr Hans Henning Atrott of Augsburg, who in the 1970s became known for founding the Germany Society for Humane Dying (Deutsche Gesellschaft für Humanes Sterben, DGHS). The DGHS, which still exists, gives expert advice on ways to commit suicide and provides suitable drugs. Atrott hit the headlines again in 1981 when he proposed to have article 216 abolished and demanded that mercy killing should be allowed if a terminally ill patient who was unable to kill himself or herself, requested it. The idea, however, had no chance in a country where euthanasia is still a dirty word.

HELMUT L. KARCHER

Netherlands

In the Netherlands it is still illegal to perform euthanasia and assisted suicide. But if doctors do so according to guidelines that are in the process of becoming law they will not be prosecuted. This is the compromise reached by the minister of justice and the parliamentary under-secretary for public health after nearly 20 years of discussion. It has been approved by the cabinet and was sent to the second chamber at the end of last year.

Basically nothing will change. What the government is doing is merely sanctioning what is already happening. A doctor who has carried out euthanasia must currently report it to the public prosecutor, who checks that the doctor has acted with 'due carefulness'. The public prosecutor checks this degree of carefulness against a list of 25 conditions, which includes consulting with a second doctor and writing a detailed report. The conditions were drawn up last year by the prosecution council in collaboration with the Royal Dutch Medical Association.

The government has reached this position only two months after the report of the Remmelink commission into euthanasia. At the time the Lubbers government was accused of setting up the commission to postpone making any decisions on the issue. The Remmelink report stated that euthanasia accounts for no more than 2 per cent of deaths a year. It reported that in 1,000 cases a year the patient did not give permission—these were mostly cases involving comatose patients or severely handicapped babies. The government believes that these cases should be brought before a judge.

The Royal Dutch Medical Association is unhappy with the government's proposal. It argues that the threat of punishment still hangs over doctors' heads. The Netherlands Association for Voluntary Euthanasia calls the government's guidelines 'extremely confusing.' According to its chairwoman, Mrs Pit Bakker, as long as euthanasia remains an offence doctors will not report it.

HANK HELLEMA

Italy

A Catholic-inspired right-to-life movement is gaining strength in Italy. A parliamentary bill for passive euthanasia has spurred the right-to-life movement, which is already campaigning against the abortion law.

The socialist parliamentarian, Loris Fortuna, whose bill led to the introduction of divorce, has proposed a bill in favour of 'passive euthanasia'.

The church considers that nature should take its course, that doctors do not necessarily have to use all means to prolong life in all circumstances. But some Italian Catholics are uneasy about Fortuna's proposal on a matter which, they claim, is difficult to define and best left to conscience.

They fear a law in favour of passive euthanasia could be the thin edge of the wedge in favour of euthanasia of those who are unfit, unintelligent or in other ways considered socially unviable. The issue has been given added edge by the decision of Milan municipality that it could no longer maintain Italy's senior novelist, 94-year-old Riccardo Bacchelli. Bacchelli, whose best known work is *The Mill on the Po*, was transferred to Monza Hospital after Milan authorities had spent US $150,000 for his maintenance. He was suffering from nothing other than old age and recognised only his 93-year-old wife.

The right-to-life movement has recently staged a series of anti-abortion demonstrations modelled on the United States anti-abortion campaign.

Japan

In April 1991 a report of a 34-year-old doctor who had given a lethal injection to a patient with cancer at Tokai University School of Medicine shocked Japan, where active euthanasia is rare.

The patient had been in hospital for four months when he developed renal failure. His family begged the medical staff to stop treating him. The doctor responsible for the 'mercy killing' did not consult his colleagues. After withdrawing treatment he gave the patient a dose of intravenous potassium chloride in the presence of one of the patient's relatives. The patient—already in a coma—had a cardiac arrest a few minutes later. Kanagawa's prefectural police have been investigating the case.

Even the Japanese Society for Dying with Dignity, which has 30,000 members, thinks that Japan is not ready to consider active euthanasia. 'It is too early, taking the spiritual climate of Japan into consideration,' said the chairman, Taneo Oki. 'We aim at passive euthanasia, which means that terminally ill patients should be allowed to die without being given treatment to keep them alive. We believe in the right to make a living will.'

According to a survey by the Japanese Medical Association in 1990, three quarters of doctors think that they should respect a patient's living will if he or she is terminally ill.

MASAYA YAMAUCHI

South Africa

Advances in medical science extend the lives of old people, and more and more old age homes are required to care for them in their reduced activity, sickness, or vegetable state.

Many elderly people indeed feel that their lives are not worth preserving. Suffering, loneliness, helplessness and the fear of becoming a burden to others are real trials in old age, even in circumstances of physical comfort and care. The subject of euthanasia—the deliberate painless ending of tormented and hopeless lives—comes up regularly, and is discussed in all its aspects. It can be seen as a sensible and humane thing, or as a dangerous opening to abuse, or simply morally wrong. Eventually perhaps we shall arrive at some agreement as to our true duty as human beings in this matter. Rather different, but surely worth consideration, is the question of allowing old but not necessarily ill people to decide for themselves when to opt out of life. Centenarians are becoming more common, but many of us in our eighth or ninth decade begin to feel we have been around long enough. We have to face the idea of sooner or later finding daily life a burden and of ourselves being a burden to others. Just as there has been produced a pill that can be used voluntarily to prevent the starting of a new life, should there not be a pill that can be used voluntarily to end an old one which is no longer of any use or joy to the owner or anyone else?

Such deaths would be free of the tragic aura of suicide. Rather would be evoked the calm philosophy of Epictetus: 'When God fails to provide for you He is giving the signal of retreat: He has opened a door, and says to you, come . . . '

Spain

In January 1985 Councillor Joseph Laporte, Health Adviser to the Catholic Government, presented the Charter of Rights of hospital patients which inter alia recognised the right of patients, in accordance with their religion and their personal beliefs, to assume responsibility, in irreversible situations, for the advent of their own death. In the words of the Councillor, 'This is not a recommendation of euthanasia, but an attempt to humanise the existence of the dying.' Councillor Laporte was formerly an eminent medical Professor in the Autonomous University, and incidentally the author of a report against smoking (much more prevalent in Spain than in Britain).

The charter gives patients the right of access to their own medical records and to have them explained by a doctor. The patient can refuse treatment if he believes it may reduce the quality of life to a degree incompatible with his own conception of personal dignity. He has the right to have risky procedures explained to him, and he must give his written consent before they are applied. The Charter sets out norms for medical conduct which have been observed for a long time, but the Provincial Government now puts its authority behind them, although not elevating them to the level of law. The Generalitat distributes the Charter, through the Catalonian Institute of Health, to all hospitals.

Even after giving his written permission for treatment the patient can retract it at any time. The Charter obliges the medical staff to maintain relations between patient and family and friends as a prime objective, but permits the patient to terminate treatment at the moment he desires. The Charter follows from one published by the Department of Health in April 1983, and it places an obligation on hospitals that wish to collaborate with the Institute of Health.

Catalonia likes to think of itself as the most advanced

province of Spain. In any case it will be interesting to see to what extent the other provinces (all very autonomous) will follow.

Switzerland

In 1988, the German-speaking Swiss Society produced a 128-page booklet, compiled by their President, Walter Baechi, to celebrate their first five years of existence. The Society has been tremendously successful in terms of membership, which stands now at 20,160.

Most doctors have come to respond positively to the Society's Living Will (*Patientenverfugungen*). The Society is prepared to take legal action against doctors who ignore it, but so far such a case has not arisen.

In 1984 the Society removed from its aims the legalisation of active euthanasia (chiefly because of the emotions aroused through the Nazi misuse of the word) and replaced it by 'assistance to very seriously ill people who want to take their own lives'. Under Swiss law anyone, including a doctor, may provide a seriously ill person with the means to end their own life, if they request this. The person giving the aid must not be a beneficiary in the suicide's will.

Much of the success of the Society has been due to the work of its Vice-President and Secretary, Dr Rolf Sigg, a Protestant Pastor of the Reformed Church. The authorities of his church have imposed sanctions on him because of this work, but Dr Sigg has said he never doubted that it was right for him to support EXIT. 'It is a matter of loving one's neighbour and showing pity.'

The society provides details of means of self-deliverance to members of at least three months' standing and, for people who have no close friends or relatives willing to be with them, it can provide someone to be there at the end. There is a moving account of an unnamed couple who did this for a 70-year-old woman who had endured 23 years of gradually increasing pain. The tablets she used were provided by her GP, who had to report the suicide to the authorities. The couple were questioned by the police, at first with hostility, but after they had seen the self-deliverance declaration, with growing understanding. 'In the end we were shown to the door with respect; they realised that two people had come a long way to a do a loving act.'

Based on a translation by Peter Johnson

United States

The defeat of Washington state's referendum on physician assisted suicide in 1991 did not resolve the core issue of the rights of terminally ill patients regarding their medical treatment. In California and Oregon voters are likely to be balloted on the euthanasia issue.

Meanwhile, a new federal law enacted in December 1991 requires any health care facility receiving funds from either the Medicaid programme for the poor or the Medicare programme for the elderly to inform adult patients of their right to refuse life sustaining medical care. They also have the right to complete a 'living will' or durable power of attorney directing the facility to withhold certain treatments.

The Patient Self Determination Act, passed by Congress in 1991, requires hospitals, hospices, home health agencies, nursing homes, and health maintenance organisations to discuss patients' wishes. It does not require the health care facility to comply with every wish.

American Medical News, an official publication of the American Medical Association, says that only between 4 per cent and 17 per cent of Americans have completed a living will or durable power of attorney, although about 70 per cent of people who die in hospitals do so after the withdrawal of life sustaining treatment.

The newspaper quotes Mary Mahowald, professor of ethics at Chicago University, as saying that care givers must still determine whether life sustaining care is futile and whether it is in the patient's best interest.

Several physicians told *American Medical News* that they were concerned that the law's requirements would interfere with the relationship between doctor and patient. In fact, the law was designed so that a patient can write an advance directive without any help from a physician.

REX RHEIN

WORLD FEDERATION OF RIGHT-TO-DIE
SOCIETIES

Australia

South Australia Voluntary Euthanasia Society (SAVES), PO Box 2151, Kent Town Centre, South Australia 5071.

Voluntary Euthanasia Society of New South Wales (VES of NSW), PO Box 25, Broadway, NSW 2007.

Voluntary Euthanasia Society of Victoria (VESV), Box 108, Mooroolbark, Victoria 3138.

West Australia Voluntary Euthanasia Society (WAVES), PO Box 7243, Cloisters Square, Perth, West Australia 6000.

Belgium

Association pour le Droit de Mourir dans la Dignité (ADMD), 55 rue du President, B-1050 Bruxelles.

Recht op Waardig Sterven (RWS), Constitutiestraat 33, 2008 Antwerp.

Canada

Dying with Dignity (DWD), 175 St Clair Avenue West, Toronto, ON, M4V 1P7.

Fondation Responsable Jusqu'à la fin (FRJF), 10150 De Bretagne, Quebec (Neufchatel), PQ, G2B 2R1.

Colombia

Fundacion Pro Derecho a Morir Dignamente (DMD), A.A. 88900, Bogotá.

Denmark

Landsforeningen Mit Livstestamente, Brondstrupvej 5, 8500 Grens.

France

Association pour le Droit de Mourir dans la Dignité (ADMD), 103 rue Lafayette, 75010 Paris.

India

The Society for the Right to Die with Dignity (SRDD), 127 Mahatma Gandhi Road, Bombay 400 023.

Israel
The Israeli Society for the Right to Die with Dignity, 116 Rotschild Bolv., Tel-Aviv, 65271.

Japan
Japan Society for Dying with Dignity (JSDD), Watanabe Bldg. 202, 2-20-1 Hongou, Bunkyoku, Tokyo 113.

Luxembourg
Association pour le Droit de Mourir dans la Dignité (ADMD-L), 50 Bd Kennedy, 4170 Esch-Alzette.

The Netherlands
Nederlandse Vereniging voor Vrijwillige Euthanasie (NVVE), 152 de Lairessestraat, Postbus 5331, 1007 AH Amsterdam.
Stichting Landelijk Besluithuis (SLB), Zuiderweg 42, 8393 KT Vinkega, Frl.

New Zealand
Voluntary Euthanasia Society (Auckland) Inc., PO Box 3709, Auckland.
Voluntary Euthanasia Society (VES), 95 Melrose Road, Island Bay, Wellington 2.

South Africa
South Africa Voluntary Euthanasia Society (SAVES), PO Box 1460, Wandsbeck 3631.

Spain
Asociacion Derecho a Morir Dignamente (DMD), Apartado 31, 134, 08080 Barcelona.

Sweden
Ratten Till Var Dod, Hoganasgatan 2 C, 753 30 Uppsala.

Switzerland
EXIT (Deutsche Schweiz) Vereinigung für humanes Sterben, CH-2540 Grenchen.

EXIT Association pour le Droit de Mourir dans la Dignité (ADMD), CP 100, CH 1222 Vesenaz, Geneva.

United Kingdom
The Voluntary Euthanasia Society (VES), 13 Prince of Wales Terrace, London W8 5PG.

The Voluntary Euthanasia Society of Scotland (VESS), 17 Hart Street, Edinburgh EH1 3RO.

United States
Americans Against Human Suffering, Inc., PO Box 11001, Glendale, CA 91206.

Concern for Dying (CFD), 250 West 57th Street, Rm 831, New York, NY 10107.

The National Hemlock Society, PO Box 11830, Eugene, OR 97440.

Society for the Right to Die (SRD), 250 West 57th Street, New York, NY 10107.

Helping Those in Distress

If someone comes to you expressing the wish to end a life that has become intolerable through illness or failing faculties, the response outlined below may help:

1 Are you sure you fully understand what is wrong with you and its probable development?

Communication between doctor and patient is not always perfect; mistaken diagnosis, though unlikely, is possible. You can change your GP (telephone or write to the local Family Practitioners' Committee: address from the phone book, local library, Community Health Council or Citizens' Advice Bureau), or ask your medical advisers to arrange for a second opinion.

2 Can you talk to relatives or friends about how you feel?

If this is difficult for you, the Samaritans (phone number in the book) will provide a sympathetic listener who will help you to think through the difficulties you face. At the very least, talking about your problem helps to clarify your own mind.

3 Are you suffering from a great deal of pain or other discomfort?

There have been great strides in recent years in controlling pain and other symptoms. You could ask to be referred to the pain clinic at your local Hospice or Hospital. Doctors have the discretion to provide adequate pain relieving medication even if this hastens the moment of death.

4 Are you apprehensive about being kept alive by medical treatment when you would prefer to be allowed to die?

The Society's Advance Directive will make your wishes plain.

5 Do you realise that, if of sound mind, you can legally refuse any item of medical treatment?

Patients often feel that they are entirely in their doctors' hands and that a less passive attitude on their part will be resented. Doctors as a whole are becoming much more willing to listen and discuss than they used to be.

The Advance Directive

The purpose of the Advance Directive is to indicate to the doctor your wishes in the event of there being no reasonable prospect of your recovery from serious illness expected to cause you severe distress or to render you incapable of rational existence.

It does not ask the doctor to do anything contrary to existing law, but should he or she be faced with a difficult decision regarding the prolongation of life in the circumstances specified, it would be helpful to him or her to know the considered opinion of the patient, expressed when in full possession of his or her faculties, and not in great pain or distress.

The law fully upholds the right of a patient to decline life-sustaining (or any other) treatment, and to receive analgesic drugs in quantities sufficient to relieve intolerable distress, and a doctor who treats a competent patient against his or her wishes commits an assault. It is the possibility that patients might not be able to express their wishes that has led to the development of Advance Directives in which the signatory directs in advance the treatment to be received or withheld in specified circumstances.

There have been two doubts about the validity of Advance Directives. The first was whether they would be upheld as legally effective by English courts in the absence of such legislation as is widespread in the USA. The second was whether doctors could be expected to act upon the directions in the document. The VES, therefore, took the opinion of Mr Alan Newman QC. The essential points he made were that the legal effectiveness of an Advance Directive depends, firstly, on the declarant's competence at the time of signing;

and, secondly, on the decision by the patient being an informed one. These two conditions mean that a patient must have sufficient understanding and intelligence to comprehend the nature, purpose and likely consequences of undergoing or refusing treatment, and the ability to communicate to the physician his or her decision in relation to the particular treatment.

The Society's form contains provisions designed to show that the declarant understood the document and signed it 'after careful consideration'. On the question of effectiveness, Mr Newman's final view was, 'Obviously until the matter has been tested in the courts, I cannot express any conclusion with certainty. Thus the necessarily tentative conclusion which I reach is that, provided the declarant is "informed" at the time when he signs the Advance Directive, such Advance Directive is effective in English law and must be followed by a doctor administering treatment to a patient who has subsequently become incompetent.'

The form should be signed and witnessed at the same time by two persons who are not relatives and who do not expect to benefit from your estate. If necessary, these witnesses could give evidence that you were of sound mind when you signed the form. If one of the witnesses were to be your doctor, it would be an advantage but it is not essential for the validity of the document. It is possible your doctor may charge a fee for this service.

One form should be given to your doctor with a request that it be placed with your medical records; you should retain a second copy. You may also wish to give a third copy to the person you judge best able to protect your interests in an emergency. Up-dating stamps are issued each year, and these should be stuck on your Advance Directive and signed, thus ensuring that your wishes regarding medical treatment at the end of life remain current.

The Voluntary Euthanasia Society also provides an Emergency Medical Treatment Card, to be signed and carried on the person. (Free to members of the Society. £1 post free to non-members.)

Statement from the British Medical Association

The BMA strongly supports the principle of an Advanced Directive which represents the patient's settled wish regarding treatment choices when the patient may be no longer able competently to express a view. The patient's refusal of specific treatments should be respected but does not imply or justify abandonment of the patient. Doctors and health care institutions should offer such medical care and pain relief as would appear acceptable to the patient and appropriate to the circumstances.

The BMA is not in favour of legally binding Advance Directives. An individual patient's rights to not supersede those of other parties, as in the case of pregnant women where there is a moral duty to another human being.

A written Advance Directive, in the absence of contrary evidence, must be regarded as representing the patient's settled opinion and doctors, having been notified of its existence, should make all reasonable efforts to acquaint themselves with its contents. In cases of emergency, however, necessary treatment should not be delayed in anticipation of a document which is not readily available.

The BMA believes that an Advance Directive can be overridden by clinical judgement in exceptional circumstances. Nevertheless, if, in an Advance Directive, the patient has expressed a clear opinion about non-treatment or discontinuing treatment, having taken medical advice and having in mind the precise clinical circumstances which now pertain, doctors should regard the patient's wishes as determinative.

Doctors with a conscientious objection to curtailing treatment in any circumstance are not obliged to comply with an Advance Directive but should advise the patient of their views and offer to step aside, transferring management of the patient's care to another practitioner.

The BMA encourages doctors to raise the subject in a sensitive manner with patients who may be thought likely to have an interest in the matter or who are anxious about the possible administration of unwanted treatments at a later stage.

Late discovery of an Advance Directive after life-prolonging treatment has been initiated is not sufficient grounds *for* ignoring it.

ADVANCE DIRECTIVE

TO MY FAMILY, MY PHYSICIAN AND ALL OTHER PER-
SONS CONCERNED

THIS DIRECTIVE is made by me _____

_____

_____

at a time when I am of sound mind and after careful consideration.

I DECLARE that if at any time the following circumstances exist,
namely:

(1) I suffer from one or more of the conditions mentioned in the
schedule; and

(2) I have become unable to participate effectively in decisions
about my medical care; and

(3) two independent physicians (one a consultant) are of the
opinion that I am unlikely to recover from illness or impair-
ment involving severe distress or incapacity for rational
existence,

THEN AND IN THOSE CIRCUMSTANCES my directions are as
follows:

1 that I am not to be subjected to any medical intervention or
treatment aimed at prolonging or sustaining my life;

2 that any distressing symptoms (including any caused by lack
of food or fluid) are to be fully controlled by appropriate
analgesic or other treatment, even though that treatment may
shorten my life.

I consent to anything proposed to be done or omitted in compliance
with the directions expressed above and absolve my medical attendants from any civil liability arising out of such acts or omissions.

I wish it to be understood that I fear degeneration and indignity far
more than I fear death. I ask my medical attendants to bear this
statement in mind when considering what my intentions would be in
any uncertain situation.

I RESERVE the right to revoke this DIRECTIVE at any time, but
unless I do so it should be taken to represent my continuing
directions.

SCHEDULE

A   Advanced disseminated malignant disease.

B   Severe immune deficiency.

C   Advanced degenerative disease of the nervous system.

D   Severe and lasting brain damage due to injury, stroke, disease or other cause.

E   Senile or pre-senile dementia, whether Alzheimer's, multi-infarct or other.

F   Any other condition of comparable gravity.

Signed _____

Date _____

WE TESTIFY that the above-named signed this Directive in our presence, and made it clear to us that he/she understood what it meant. We do not know of any pressure being brought on him/her to make such a directive and we believe it was made by his/her own wish. So far as we are aware we do not stand to gain from his/her death.

Witnessed by:

Signature: _____   Signature: _____

Name: _____   Name: _____

Address: _____   Address: _____

_____   _____

_____   _____